IT DOES HAPPEN TO MEN

By James Mackie

A diary of abuse by a male survivor

Contents

PART 1 – Prologue

- Introduction
- What did I do
- Backstory
- Marriage and kids
- Make up your own mind

PART 2 – The Diary

- A diary kept for almost a year with records of incidents and feelings written as they happened

PART 3 – Epilogue

- Why did I stop the diary then?
- What happened next?
- The legal system
- 18 months later
- The Internet and the affair
- Love bombing
- Escape plan
- Life is too short
- The escape
- The result
- What is domestic abuse
- What to do if you are suffering
- What is Narcissistic Personality Disorder (NPD)
- What are the Types of Narcissist and How to spot them
- How to get out – planning and support

PART 1 – PROLOGUE

Introduction

Some time ago, towards the end of July 2013, after an aggressive attack on me by my wife, I decided that I was going to start to record the pattern of behaviour and what she did. I wanted to do this, so I could present it to her to show her that something was wrong and then she might do something about it. That was my plan, my thoughts behind starting to record what happened and when. Simple really: gather the evidence, show it to her and she will realise what she's doing and change. Then all will be well, and we will be happily married ever after. Or so I thought. Is that what happened? Not exactly. What did happen? Well, you'll have to read it to believe it.

I thought that my wife's outbursts of verbal and physical abuse were down to hormones and perhaps followed her monthly cycle. I thought that a dose of HRT or something would sort her out and then we'd get the 'nice' wife and mother back all the time. Whilst at times I hated her following an attack, it is how she treated me and the children that I really hated. I had always thought I loved her and cared for her but maybe I was just dependent on her and on gaining her approval at every turn.

What I did.

I recorded most, but not all, incidents over the following year in the calendar app on my phone. After the attack mentioned before I was away on business for a few days and I synchronised all those notes to my laptop. I spent a long time late into the early hours of the 4th of July cutting and pasting each of the notes and every diary entry into a single document.

Doing this that night changed everything for me. My understanding of how things were crumbled right in front of me.

By opening, reading and cataloguing every incident in my log my eyes were truly opened to the extent of what had been going on. It wasn't her being just horrible, nasty and shouting at me – it breached often into violence and was extended to the children too - mostly my eldest but also the little one.

This was not normal behaviour – even though I had just accepted it as normal for us. I suppose it was just such a big part of our everyday lives that it seemed normal to us. I suddenly realised that it was not normal, that it was not acceptable, and I really did wake up to the reality of the situation.

The children and I were spending our lives wondering which Caroline we would get when we faced her. Would it be the nice, kind version that we so craved for or would it be the nasty vicious and angry one we dreaded? We spent our time answering her challenging questions, not with the truth, but with what we believed would be the answer that she needed to hear. The answer that gave the least line of resistance or the least reaction from her. We spent our days and nights walking around on eggshells, waiting for the next outburst to hit us, trying desperately not to provoke it or cause it.

We thought that if only we did everything she wanted us to do, or perhaps more correctly, if we did what she ordered us to do, then we would get her approval, and everything would be ok. Then there would be no shouting or worse. Except it was hardly ever ok. It didn't matter what we did, it was impossible to please her all the time and to do exactly everything the way she wanted it or to meet her exacting levels of expectation. I could do a million things around the house, leaving her practically nothing to do but she would still be able to find the one tiny thing that was not perfect or had been missed. Then she would go mad and I would suffer. We would all suffer.

Backstory

How we met was not the ideal of circumstances. Caroline and I first met in a pretty little seaside town in the South of England called Lyme Regis in the late 90's. We were both in our mid 20's and we were starting out our careers as trainees in our first real jobs after university. When I first met Caroline I already had a girlfriend. She was living and working back in Wales where I am originally from at the time, so she wasn't around. I met Caroline through a friend of my girlfriend. A girl called Frances who was moving into a shared house in the town and I helped her move into that house. I had a car and she didn't, so I offered to help her out.

Caroline was living in the shared house that she moved into. She was there the night I moved her in and so we met. My first impressions of Caroline were that she was pretty, nice, seemed sweet and actually quite my type with long dark hair.

Over the next few months Caroline and I became good friends. We often went out with Frances and some other friends but after a while we started going places just the two of us. It was completely plutonic on my part, but she might have had other ideas. Me being me, I just couldn't see it and never thought she would be interested in me. Then one night, about 6 months after meeting her, she invited me around to hers, so she could cook a meal for me. When I got there, she was all dressed up and I discovered that we had the whole house to ourselves. This was the night before I was due to go back home to see my girlfriend in Wales, so it was a nice gesture, or at least that's what I was thinking at the time.

We drank plenty of alcohol, in fact she made me a pint of vodka and coke which meant that I wasn't going to be driving anywhere. The food was terrible, a right disaster and we had a good laugh about that. Then we settled down to watch a film and after a while of watching and talking away she leant over and kissed me.

I say she kissed me and well she did and then she was practically all over me. What did I do? I was shocked as I could not read the signs and just thought we were friends. I didn't think she was into me, I have never been able to work that out and, so I did what any man would do when a pretty girl turns it up a notch. I went with the flow and carried on, I responded. After a while she said, "shall we go up then?" and led me to her bedroom and her bed.

We had sex. It wasn't great, and it wasn't love making. It was sex, but it was rather strange as she seemed to have no rhythm or flow. Later, I found out that she was a virgin, but I had no idea at the time. She had no idea what to do which made sense really.

The next day I went away to see my girlfriend in Wales and had a pretty good time. It was May and the weather was good. She was working some of the time, but we went out, had fun, went to the beach, had great sex in her flat and enjoyed our time together. I did however feel guilty and knew that I wanted my girlfriend but also that I had somehow ruined that. I had a strange feeling when I left her to head home, the feeling that it was the last time I would see her. In fact, I *knew* it was the last time and I was right. It was the last time I ever saw her. I was so sad and upset leaving her that time. She was the love of my life at that point and I just wanted to be with her.

When I got back to Lyme Regis, Caroline came over to see me and I told her I did not want to break up with my girlfriend and so finished our 'affair'. I remember being rather cruel and saying, I must make a choice between love and practicality and as I'm a romantic I choose love. Meaning that she was just a convenience and I really loved my girlfriend.

Somehow though we made up and got together again and this time we spent all our time together and even the sex was better and constant, normally at my place. On a Sunday morning after she had spent the night over at my place, she wanted to know what I was doing that day. I said I was just going to see my Grandfather who lived not far away in Exeter and she took offence at this as I was not overtly inviting her as I'd said I was going not we. She stormed out and walked herself back home and that was it, we broke up. Looking back this was a big red flag but I could not see it at the time.

Soon after my girlfriend also broke up with me due to the distance and the fact that we struggled to find a way to be together. But I also think she had been tipped off about me and Caroline by Frances. So, I went from having two girls on the go to none. I was bad.

Then about 6 weeks later after not seeing Caroline at all, I saw her as I drove near her house for work one day. Next thing I knew she left a note on my car at work saying, "so you're still alive then?". That night I went around to her place, we immediately hugged and kissed and that was it, we were back on.

She was pretty, nice, had a good job and prospects, educated, funny and so I thought 'why not? We have fun together'. Looking back there were a few red flags as to her behaviour but I just never realised. The storming out, the taking advantage of someone who's already in a relationship with someone else and then breaking up and leaving a note on my car.

At the time, I had no indication at all of what was yet to come.

Marriage and Kids

2 years later, after having lived together for a year and moving around a bit with work, we settled in North Yorkshire then we married in June 2000. I remember asking her to marry me at about 3am in the night after some makeup sex after an argument. It was a Valentines night less than a year after we had got together, and we had been out with our best friends for a joint meal. I said will you marry me, and she said, "go on then". It was funny at the time.

Our first child, Sacha was born after 3 years of marriage and our second, Alice, 3 years after that. Throughout our relationship and these years together she was very bossy – making all the decisions and always telling me what to do. I was modern in my outlook and did my fair share of housework, actually I did most of it, and most of the cooking. However, it didn't really matter what I did because it was never quite good enough.

Over time, little by little, she seemed to work things in a way that I stopped playing golf and football and going out with friends or work colleagues. It wasn't obvious that this was happening, it was very subtle. Arguments, sulks and moods when I was doing things, putting conditions on them such as, 'if you want to do this then you need to go early and be back by such and such a time or you can't go'. If I was late I'd get a hard time, grilled and shouted at. Golf with my dad on Sunday morning started at first light and I needed to be back by 9-10 for when she would wake up. It was just so difficult that in the end I stopped doing things and after a few years I had no activities or friends outside of our mutual circle. Contacts at work were restricted to work time only. If I had to be away on business for work she always made such a fuss, and I'd have to do so much around the trip to make sure she had meals and all things were done. It made it all so hard and at times and it really affected my work because I'd always avoid staying away.

I had to get permission for anything and everything. If I wanted to do something it would result in an argument, unrealistic conditions or both. Our finances were shared and although she did not fully 'control' it all, I was not really allowed to spend or buy anything without her approval. If I did, it was always wrong and would result in an argument and shouting so I would then buy things for myself in secret and hide them. Eventually she would notice and moan, but I'd just say I had them for ages.

Every now and again she would want to sit down and completely go through our finances and money and itemise everything. She was always focussed on money and us always having savings just in case. She was a real worrier.

People at work always perceived that I was 'under the thumb' and 'controlled', that she wore the trousers at home, and that she was really bossy, but I doubt anyone would have believed the extent of how she treated me. In our early time together and for a long time during our marriage she was the main earner and so she always had that hold on me which meant I had to do more and please her. It took me more than 6 years after meeting her to get to the point where I earned more than she did and that was only because she went part-time. She never seemed to have the full respect for me as an equal and as a husband. She was always in charge and what she said went.

When our daughter was born in 2003, it was the first time she started to get quite anxious about germs and sterilising the baby's bottle. It was sensible hygiene, but she was always over the top about it. If a bottle was left too long around after sterilising, then it had to be poured away and restarted.

Sacha was fed only organic and free-range food for about the first 5 years. Caroline became obsessed about the food being organic and I now realise this was the start of her obsessive illness that developed slowly over the next few years into fully blown OCD (obsessive compulsive disorder). Sacha was not allowed any sweets or anything 'bad' for her. All this for several years and some even to this day.

We tried to move to a new house several times over several years, for work or just for a nicer house. I think we were notorious amongst estate agents in the area as right at the last minute, just before a sale was due to go ahead, she would get cold feet and pull out leaving buyers and sellers in a mess. Big changes of any sort always seemed to cause her major stress and anxiety. Eventually we did move in to a lovely house in a nice town called Richmond which not far from where we were living at that time. However, the first night we had the keys she said she hated the place and wanted to stop the whole sale. But it was too late in the day for that and so for the first 3 nights we slept at my parents' house, which was very close until she calmed down.

When Sacha was about 18 months old, she was desperate for another baby. She did get pregnant quite easily but had a couple of early miscarriages which was not easy to deal with. Then when Sacha was 3 she did get pregnant and it was going well except that she became very sick. She had very bad morning sickness and afterwards it was diagnosed as possibly HG (hyperemesis gravidarum), a condition that is like morning sickness all day every day and ten times the strength of normal morning sickness. During this whole time, I did all the work in the house, cooked all the meals, took Sacha to and from school, made sure Caroline had food and running back and forth between home, work and Sacha's school. After about week 11 week she decided she felt too bad and too sick to continue with the pregnancy. Without discussing at all with me, she booked an abortion. She even made me drive her to the clinic. I had no choice really as she threatened to go on her own anyway and I couldn't let her do that. So, I took her to Leeds to an abortion clinic and she went in the place alone. I stayed outside. I saw a church and I went in and I prayed. I prayed properly for what was then the first time in several years asking God to stop her from doing it. Next thing I knew she came out and had not done it. She had changed her mind. She decided that she couldn't go through with it. I was so relieved and thankful.

However, only a week later we were back at the abortion clinic in Leeds again and that time she went through with it. She aborted, got rid of, killed our baby. I cried for days. Guess what though. She blamed me and said it was my fault as I was not supportive enough whilst she was feeling sick.

That was the point I think, that our marriage died.

It was never the same after that and even though I still thought I loved her, something inside me died and that was the love I had for her. I was never able to look at her or feel for her the way as I did before that point. It took me a long time to be able to look her properly in the eyes. This also meant that I was less likely to do what she said all the time which then also increased the friction. I lost my respect for her and so the arguments and her subsequent behaviour started to get worse.

After that she felt guilty and started obsessing about having a baby to replace the one she 'lost'. This is what she told people and made me tell people, that she had lost the baby again. That it was another miscarriage. I think only one person knew the actual truth. Everyone was so sympathetic, but I think she never got over the guilt, even to this day. She did so much research on HG and saw a few specialists for advice. She found out about drugs that would help if she was ill again in pregnancy and then she got pregnant again.

Her next pregnancy was an awful period. She was sick, and she made my life hell. But somehow, we got through it. Afterwards, again she said I was not supportive despite doing everything humanly possible.

When Alice was born, all seemed ok for a while. She was hard work as a baby, but we loved her so much. She was special and precious. We might never have had her as we thought we would always have stuck at two which made her so loved. When she was 6 months old, Caroline's father who had not been well passed away. I think that hit her hard too, and during that period she started to develop further problems with OCD relating to germs and getting sick.

Over time she developed such phobia about vomiting or feeling nauseous again and couldn't stand the thought of feeling sick at all. From there she developed OCD to such a degree that it greatly affected the lives of our entire family. Anything from outside was deemed 'contaminated' and so had to be cleaned and wiped with an anti-bacterial wipe – this included all shopping and food bought at say a supermarket. If I did anything with raw chicken for example, then everything had to be cleaned down at least twice with antibacterial spray because it spreads salmonella everywhere seemingly. There were so many rules and counter rules that it was ridiculous and impossible to live with.

If someone visited our house the place had to be spotless and perfect for them coming and then disinfected and fully cleaned after they had gone. It caused such a fuss and arguments that we hardly ever had anyone round – this extended even to our Nanny Karen, who had been with us for about 4 years by that time. Low and behold anyone who walked through the house with outdoor shoes on as she would go mental at them. Once our best friends' daughter walked through the conservatory and into the kitchen from outside with her shoes on and Caroline screamed at her making her scared and cry.

If we went to the doctors' surgery or dentist, then we had to change our clothes and have a shower the second we got in.

She used separate car and clothes for work and they were never mixed. These rules were not always explained, many were just in her head but if you broke one then your life was hell.

Make up your own mind

So that's some background information about the relationship and family life for us all. There were plenty of 'red flags' as to her way of thinking and her behaviour but I had overlooked them. I didn't know what red flags were or what they might lead to. They are just signals that show types of behaviour demonstrated by people who are not all that they appear, not quite normal.

She was my wife and I believed that we should work hard to make the marriage work for us and for the children most of all. So, I just got on with it. I accepted my lot and did my best or at least that's what I thought at the time.

Hindsight is a great thing, but you cannot change the past nor predict the future with a degree of certainty. You can only live in the here and now and that was all I was doing.

Read the diary and make up your own mind.

All these events captured, actually happened. Nothing here is made up or embellished. They were noted straight after each incident in a quiet moment on my phone diary. Read on.

PART 2 – THE DIARY

Intro

The wonders of technology. I turned 35 and I got a great smartphone as my present to myself (with her permission of course) when things began to kick off.

I always had my phone on me and it was perfect to use to note down incidents and notes of what happened. I just used the notes section in the calendar app. On each day I recorded the events as and when they happened. Many notes were written down in pure frustration and anger, it was my way of not only recording the incidents but a release of pent up feelings and a way to reduce my reaction to her. You will see from the content.

Sometimes I just say what happened, other times I expand into my thoughts and feelings and generally it's in the middle.
I noted all these things down for a year and when I finally copied and pasted them into a full document I could not believe what I was reading. The quantity of incidents against me was far more than I had realised.
However, greater than that was the realisation of the extent

that the children were reeled in and subjected to the behaviour. At the time of starting the diary the kids were aged 10 and 4.

At the end of the diary I will explain what my next steps were. So, hang in there.

July

July 25th 2013 8.00 am

I have now decided to start recording all the details of my wife's behaviour pattern. I am going to use my phone and keep notes in the notes section of the diary.

She has always been a pre-menstrual nut job, but it is getting worse and she will not accept it or recognise it at all in any way. She always refuses to take any responsibility for her actions and she never ever apologises for anything. In the end it's always me apologising just to keep the peace and try to move on. She does not see anything wrong in her actions and maybe if I can present the evidence she may be able to.

She always says it is me, that I'm the one in the wrong - yet she is the one who gets violent - I just shout and swear more out of frustration at being treated like some idiot all the time and bullied by her.

Yes, that's it. I am being bullied and abused - I can't believe I just acknowledged that??!! For the first time I realise that I am being bullied and more than, that it's abusive behaviour by her.

How can you hit someone or shout at someone for 30 minutes because of some minor thing and say it's not you but them? It makes no sense. I'm at a total loss as to what to do.

July 25th 2013 12.10pm

Caroline slapped me on the face and scratched me on the arms during an argument after 30 minutes of shouting at me. It's just a normal episode.

I do something wrong and then she starts shouting and berating me. Eventually I shout back and then she will do something to up the level. This time a slap and a scratch, maybe she is trying to provoke me when she does this so that I'm in the wrong. That way she can exercise more control over me. Or maybe I'm just reading too much into it and she just has anger and control issues?

Anyway, it's not good and it's not fun for me. I am always on the defensive, always waiting for what is coming next. It doesn't matter what the cause is. It's always something minor that I have either done or not done and could be anything. It's so confusing to deal with.

July 30th 2013 9.25 am

She went mad again, shouting at me and the kids and then when Alice was naughty she chased her downstairs and grabbed her really roughly by the arm and manhandled her.

She wasn't doing this in gest. She had that crazy, angry look about her and was not in any way gentle with her. So, I stepped in and took her away from her to protect her. It's what I have always done or tried to do. And then she turns on me.

When I took her away from her she went even madder, shouting and hitting me. Then she started shouting at Sacha for no real reason other than her being the next easy target. Then her focus turned back to me and she shouted at me saying the house is a mess because she didn't do any tidying up, and she does all the work. Rather odd that she does all the work, but didn't tidy up?

This has been a common theme. Even though I do all the cooking, ironing, hoovering and clean the bathrooms; I apparently do nothing, and she does it all. Plus, the things that I do, are complete rubbish in her opinion and not up to standard – her phrase is 'slap dash'. I'm good for nothing apparently.

July 31st 2013 00.45am

She started shouting at me because I had not finished tidying and setting up the spare back bedroom for my parents coming. She was complaining about not having a shower, something about the bath mat, and going on and on like she does. Saying the same thing again and again, provoking me.

Then she started going on about toilet roll, telling me I had to go out to get some from the supermarket now, after midnight. She was really winding me up and trying to push my buttons. She started hitting me again and at that point I nearly cracked. I shouted a lot and slammed the door and I am not proud of it, but I raised my fists at her but did not hit her. I managed to control myself and hold back but I have no idea how. She just pushes and pushes. I'm scared one day I will crack and just lay her out. She chooses to pick moments when you are tired and least expecting it to go on the attack. Like this just when I was going to sleep.

After that she followed me wherever I went. If I moved to one room, or another part of the house to get away from her, she'd just follow me. Going on and on about the same things again and again until after 1 in the morning. Absolutely crazy and out of order for no real reason. No one deserves to be treated like this.

August

August 9th 2013 21.00

I was working away down in London at this point in time, which was my Godsend. Being away a few nights a week helped me a lot. However, I was never off the hook as she could call me.

She rang me up at 7pm going mad about the mops and asking me which one was which and that she needed to mop the floor because my dad had tramped throughout the house with his outdoor shoes on. Yes, he wore shoes in the house and so that's my fault as is the fact she doesn't know which mop is which.

So, two things about this, one is that we have separate mops for the bathrooms and toilets and for the rest of the house. This is part of her OCD issues. Secondly my mum and dad were staying at our house to look after the kids during the summer holidays to save us childcare and my dad was actually painting the outside windows of our house. He was helping us and doing us a favour.

A short while later she rang me back, shouting at me asking about how to extend the mop so she could use it properly. She was saying her back was hurting and shouting at me because she couldn't do it and was using it in its short-closed form. Like it was my fault she couldn't do it. It was one of those mops with a telescopic handle and so you just twist it to make it longer or shorter but she couldn't work that out and so it was again my fault.

She then rang me again at 8.30pm going on at me for half an hour about my dad tramping through, having to clean and mop the floor and do everything plus moaning about my parents being there and not helping etc. She was always negative about my parents and saying really bad things about them. They kept their distance because of her but would always help and support whenever I asked. These were all a repeat of things that she had said on the previous two calls. Is that normal? I think not.

She rang me yet again at 9pm about a minute after getting off the phone from the previous call, shouting at me about a bath mat being next to towels and a mattress protector on top of some bedding. No real idea what the problem was but again it was all from her OCD issues. In the end I put the phone down and when she rang back I didn't answer, so she left a not very nice message telling me off for those things in the airing cupboard and telling me to wash it all at the weekend. I let her mum hear the message and she was appalled at the calls she was making to me and the things she was saying. She said Caroline had always been wild and badly behaved and that I shouldn't put up with this behaviour. It's funny how her mum knew how bad she was, knew how badly she treated me but never said or did anything to Caroline.

August 23rd 2013 18.45 – France

We were on holiday in Spain and she started shouting at me because she was emptying the dishwasher and doing all the work when it should be me doing it all. Then she hit me in the chest and face and tweaked my nipples hard digging her nails in. She then stormed away and sat down eating chocolate and not saying anything for several hours, leaving me to finish doing all the work in cleaning up the kitchen and tidying the place.

August 24th 07.50am

Again, she went on and on moaning and shouting at me for any little thing for about 20 minutes until I went out to the supermarket for bread. A nice pleasant walk down to the local bakers to get bread and cakes and escape the noise and rubbish. It was a common thing for me, looking for an escape. Anything to get away from her and her incessant whinging.

Later she shouted at me for taking too long getting dressed, for not putting on the dishwasher at night the night before and for leaving my shoes by the door. All amazingly terrible things that I had done.

Other than these two incidents, for once the holiday passed rather peacefully. Sometimes we can have some good times together.

September

September 17th 08.30am

Caroline rang me at work at 8.30 in the morning to nag me for using the wrong or old soya milk for cooking the fish pie last night and to go on at me for not feeding the cat before I left at 5am. No 'hello how are you, did you get to London ok?' or anything like that, just launching in at me. Bearing in mind I get up at 4.30 to drive to London for work.

Then she shouted at me for not doing anything in the mornings and abdicating it all to her. Another of her favourite jibes. Saying I abdicate responsibility of all work and leave it for her. Except when I'm there I do it all but when I'm not its physically impossible. What am I expected to do at 4.30 in the morning? What is she on about?

September 17th 20.00

She asked Sacha to empty the dishwasher. Sacha then decided to ask for a £1 if she unloaded the dishwasher. Funny girl was chancing it but was actually making a point in that her friends do get pocket money for doing chores and so if she did things she should get some pocket money. But all it did was provoke the raging bull; Caroline. She went mad at her just for asking.

Caroline then proceeded to shout at her for around 20 minutes and finished it off by slapping Sacha on the bare back, leaving a nice red hand print on it. At the same time saying things like her room was a mess and she never helps etc. It was awful, and I felt powerless to stop it all. I felt so bad for Sacha, she was just being defiant.

October

October 5th 2013 19.00

Caroline went mad at me because we had had a builder round and she had the tutor also in the house and she can't cope with it as they make the house dirty. It was only two visitors but of course they are dirty, and it sets her OCD anxieties off. She always gets anxious then and ends up losing it if people come to the house. We really have had to stop inviting people over because of her over the top reactions and anxiety. Even we have to change our clothes from outdoor to indoor clothes the minute we come home.

October 15th 2013 07.00am

She went mad at me because I didn't get Alice dressed before I left for work, even though she had said to me the night before just to get everyone breakfast and then go to work. She would do it when she got up.

She shouted and swore at me in front of Alice to which Alice repeated "f*** off", which made her even madder. What do you expect? If you swear in front of kids, then they will pick it up and copy it. Alice is only 4 after all. She was the one that swore, not me. Yet it's my fault she repeated her words.

October 15th 2013 18.00

She went mad and shouted at me all because she came home from work and I had not got her tea all ready for her for when she came in. I was going out to take the kids to their school disco and so she would have to get her own tea. Reckon even if I had made her something there would have been something wrong with it anyway. She was just looking for a fight. So, I left with the kids and escaped to their disco.

October 18th 2013 19.35

She rang me when I was in the car driving back from London and said "Where are you" in a really nasty voice. This was a pretty common thing for her to do. If I was a little late she would be calling and asking where I was, and this was not out of concern for me.

When I told her I was still around 30 minutes or so from home she shouted, "bloody hell, you'll only be back at 8 o'clock" and then slammed the phone down on me. No attempt to ask why I was late, was there an accident or bad traffic or something, no, just abuse. I was driving a 2-3-hour journey home after a full day's work and leaving home at 5.00am to get to work in the first place. Sometimes traffic is bad, and I get held up.

When I got home she ignored me the whole rest of the night and went to bed. She only eventually spoke to me very late on when I brought her a cup of tea. Again, a peace offering from me to smooth things over. The usual pattern.

Oct 20th 2013 22.00

Tonight, she has been going on at me and moaning at me for every little thing. Moaning about a plumber coming around and making me cancel it as she couldn't face someone coming into the house due to her OCD issues as usual.

The next subject was her going on about the previous Tuesday again, when we had the tutor and builder round at the same time and this being such a terrible act of who knows what. Then about me having a friend of Alice's and his Mum coming around to the house on Friday – again a heinous crime. My daughter has a friend.

And then all about the cloth I was using to clean the kitchen down with, seemingly it was not a brand new clean one and so I'd be spreading germs around – another OCD issue. Every cloth had to be new each day and everything had to be wiped with antibacterial wipes as well.

Again, she moaned about the fact we have run out of kitchen roll and I didn't buy enough from the Cash & Carry and that I haven't joined the Cash & Carry membership yet and got my card even though I worked near to them. And that she always buys toiletries from Superdrug and organises all of the household toiletry things which I don't do. But she has a loyalty card so of course she buys it all.

Then she was going on at me about being more organised in the morning and saying that she won't do nothing in the morning any longer and I have to do it all now. Like she does anything anyway.

Like that's a bloody surprise, as when I am there she does nothing and sits on her fat bum on the sofa on the bloody Internet stuffing her face with chocolate and telling me what to do.

Not only that but she is frigid. We have had sex twice since Alice was born - she is 4 now and both times was the night before a hospital appointment when she needed the feedback on it due to the tear - and then it was like shagging a sack of spuds and lifeless ones at that.

What a farce of a marriage I feel like a slave.

Rant over!!!

October 21st 2013 08.00

This morning she moaned at me for kneeling down on the ground with my suit trousers on as they are of course dirty – OCD issues again. All I did was kneel down on the ground to do my shoe laces but as my trousers are worn outside it seems they are all 'infected' with germs. By kneeling down, I transfer them to the floor in the house and we could all DIE!!!!!

No thanks at all for the cup of tea I made the night before or breakfast made that morning before work. I never get thanks for anything. I can do so much and all I get is moaned at for something that I may have not done or not up to her expected standard. Sometimes there are things completely in her head that she never communicated to me in any way, so how would I have known to do them? This is impossible.

October 23rd 2013 19.00

Today I have been shouted at for doing some of my work whilst I was helping Sacha with her PowerPoint project for school. Seemingly I am not allowed to do any work at home and must focus only on Sacha – despite having numerous issues at work and demanding emails from my boss. My boss is a nutter too by the way. I am having to deal with a new boss who is so demanding and controlling, telling me what to do all the time and on my back always. Sending emails at all hours and expecting an immediate response. Two crazies in my life, this is going to kill me for sure.

Then later on she rang me on my mobile shouting at when I was sent out to the shops by her to get some things we needed and a newspaper. This was because she had just remembered last minute about some Lego deal offer she wanted that was in the newspaper. It seems that I was taking too long doing her errands for her.

When I got back home she shouted at me because I had been out for a whole 20 minutes doing the shopping she sent me out to do. In the time I was out, whilst with her and in her care, their mother, both the kids had been naughty, and Alice did a wee on a pushy toy dog. It was one of those sit on, furry, almost real looking toy dogs.

She continued to shout at me saying all I had done all day was take Alice to football training and stand there for 2 hours and then do some work on the computer?! Never mind the fact I had made lunch and tea for everyone and gone shopping twice at her request.

She shouted at me, telling me I'd have to wash the floor tonight as Alice walked through it with wet socks that were covered in wee after she had done the wee on the dog. It was all quite funny really and I was desperately trying not to laugh because if I had I am sure I'd get a good slap or more.

It just proves that she can't cope with the children, even for just 20 minutes in her care. She relies on me for the kids' discipline, homework as well as almost everything else. Now I don't do everything, but I do a hell of a lot. I'm pretty sure I do more than most men and its certainly not shared out even 50/50. I reckon I do 70% of household chores and things to do with the kids. But it's never good enough. I am never good enough and she never ceases to make sure I know this. Is she trying to break me?

She is a pre, post and during menstrual nightmare - I have told her she needs to go to the doctor about it, but she won't - she thinks she is perfect and that it is all me. That all the issues are because of me and I just need to do more to make everything ok and her happy. Everything is my fault and she takes no responsibility for her actions or behaviour. She never apologises. To make her happy, according to her, is for me to do exactly what she wants when she wants it. Also, for me to do that to her exacting standards and whims.

At least she hasn't hit me yet this month - just a few days to survive and maybe we'll get the other Caroline back. For a couple of weeks at least before it all starts again. A vicious cycle it seems. Nice for a few days, then nasty. If I just take it then nice for a few days, then nasty again. If I react and fight back or argue then its nastier, sulk and silent treatment until I apologise and do more to make up for it, then it's nice for a while before something sends her back to nasty. Maybe it's nothing at all to do with her menstrual cycle and PMT?

October 24th 2013 09.30am

Caroline went mad shouting at me because I had not emptied the dishwasher yet that morning. That didn't mean I was not going to do it just that I had not done it when she expected it to be done. Also shouted at because I didn't mop the floor before I went to bed last night after the terrible Pushy Dog Pee Gate scandal. Shouting at me in my face for about half an hour!!!

October 24th 2013 13.30

Went mental shouting at us because Sacha wanted help with her homework and had asked her for help. It was a Farmland project and she was saying to me that I never ever help with any of the kid's homework ever. Although I'm pretty sure I do and did even the other day looking back at my diary. Never is a word she often throws in. I never do this, or I never do that, just because I didn't once or the most recent time. Then also she uses the word always a lot. I always make a mess, I always shout at her, I always take too long, I always do things slapdash or rubbish.

Then she shouted at me to now stop cleaning the kitchen and when I didn't come to her immediately and quickly enough she screamed at me in my face. She grabbed my arm and dug her nails into it, scratching and drawing blood and then she punched me in the chest 3 or 4 times - all this in front of the kids. This wasn't playful or light punching but full on chest punches with the most awful scary and vicious look on her face plus screaming at the same time. I just stood there and took it. I have no idea how.

Then a while later after she had gone away, and it was all quiet again, I was in the conservatory with Sacha doing her school work with her and she came back to have another go at me. I had to lock the door and lock us in the conservatory as she was screaming, and I was so scared she was going to attack me again. She went away giving up after a while.

About fifteen minutes later Alice spilt some flour on the carpet and she went mad shouting at her and calling her stupid. She is a 4-year-old girl and so sweet and she should not be called stupid. It's the kind of thing that would undermine her whole confidence. No wonder he has a slight stutter. She is probably scared to speak half the time.

Just when I had thought I'd escaped this month without getting hit! I had a weird out of body experience where I could see me just hitting her back but really managed to keep relatively calm and not retaliate. I do think this diary helps. It was a thought that lingered in my head but stopped there. I didn't act on it and I think writing this down is helping me keep a lid on my reactions. However, my lack of reaction seems to be making her up the level of shouting and abuse. It's like she wants me to react. She needs me to fight back and when I don't she doesn't know what to do.

October 25th 2013 09.45

She shouted at me for leaving the dirty washing basket in the wrong place on the floor in the kitchen and for putting the clothes dryer in the wrong place in the landing. What a disaster?! They have to be placed in exactly the right spot as they are dirty or contaminated in some way. It's another OCD rule that has evolved for some reason. This OCD is getting out of hand, yet she will not admit it. If I bring up the subject, she just loses it and says I must just follow her rules. Saying that if I loved her I would just do it and not argue or resist. I think that's emotional blackmail, a tactic she seems to use a lot.

October 26th 2013 09.00

Caroline went mad at me again. This time it was because I had not packed everything and what I did pack was not done right for us all going to her mums for the first time since Alice was born. I was the one doing all the packing, but it was not good enough. A pattern repeated often in different situations.

October 27th 2013 08.00am

We arrived at her mothers in London and stayed overnight. She started losing it the minute she woke up because yesterday she saw her mum had some sort of infection on her leg and had walked barefoot around her house.

Suddenly, because of this, her mother's house is now full of contagious germs and we had to pack up and leave there and then and head home. We were supposed to be staying 2-3 days with her mother. We stayed about 12 hours in the end and it's a 3 hour journey each way.

When we got home we all had to change clothes immediately and have a bath or shower. First though before we could even go in the house, I had to enter and go get new socks for everyone, so they could walk in the house. OCD on another level.

Everything that was taken with us needed to be wiped with antibacterial wipes as they are full of germs - this is nowadays quite normal if we have been out somewhere but especially somewhere like a hospital or the doctors - OCD gone mad.

I also have had to leave all bags and everything else in the car as it all needs wiped down and she couldn't face doing it now. I'm talking everything needs to be wiped and all clothes, even if they have not been worn or even out of the suitcase, have now to be boil washed.

I had to take the other car to get some fish and chips for us to eat as if I'd gone in the people carrier now. After I had been in it earlier with the clothes on that I'd worn at her mum's house, my new changed clothes would be contaminated, and I would have to wash them and have another shower again!

October 27th 2013 23.20

Tonight, she started going crazy because on Monday she has a special offer day at Sainsburys where she works at and both kids are off school which makes it all too difficult.

Then, as she got up, she kicked over and smashed my glass that I put on the floor, so it was my fault she kicked it over.

She went mental at me shouting at me and then kicked me in the thigh shouting that she did the same thing last week and I should put empty glasses on the worktop and not leave them on the floor.

Why do I stay with this woman - she makes my life a misery and gives me no pleasure at all – ever. How can I love her? One of the weird marvels of humanity, or do I just think I love her as I have no other choice? I just don't know. This is no life, this is confusing. She makes it so hard and so confusing I just don't know what to do.

If she just said sorry to me some of the time for her actions, or maybe even just once it might make a small difference, but she never does. It's always me who has to apologise even though it is normally not my fault. Even though it's her fault or in her head, it's me that always makes the peace.

October 28th 2013 11.00

I had to cancel a visit to my uncle and my sister as Caroline did not want to drive over to Harrogate just to sit in an old person's house watching TV. She overlooks the fact that we are visiting for them, to see them and for them to see the kids. My Uncle is old and very important to me, but she cannot see beyond her own selfishness.

It's very similar reasons as to why we have not visited my parents and grandad in Wales. She sees my family as being dirty and horrible and doesn't want to stay with them and can't be bothered driving all that way. It makes no difference what it means to them, me or our kids. It's all about her feelings. Sometimes when she is ranting and shouting at me she says the most awful things about my parents and family. She is pretty much the same about her own mother a lot of the time.

She also can't stand any of them, including her own mother visiting us and staying over so they don't come now. Except for earlier this year in the summer school holidays where we needed them to look after the kids and that was a total nightmare.

October 28th 2013 20.00

Today I have been shouted at or nagged for:

- Not doing a good enough shopping list

- Arranging to go and see my Uncle and Sister who is visiting him

- Putting Alice in the pyjamas that she wore at her mother's despite being washed on a boil wash to decontaminate them

Also, today I had to take Sacha to the dentist and she had to put on old clothes before we went and then get changed again into indoor clothes when we got back. This OCD and the rules are just expanding and changing by the day.

November

November 6th 2013 14.00

I was outside in the garden and heard Caroline screaming at Sacha in the conservatory. I looked in the window and saw Caroline hit Sacha on the head. It was all about something to do with homework, but she was going mental at her.

She turned on me and started shouting at me when I came in and I have no idea as to why or what it was all about.

A while later Caroline kicked Sacha in the bum and hurt her just as Sacha was going up the stairs to her bedroom. There was absolutely no need for this. I shouted at Caroline to get way and I stayed and comforted Sacha. This is so confusing for Sacha as her mum is like this to her one minute then all nice as pie the next. It's bad enough for me but it's awful for a 10-year-old.

November 9th 08.05

I was away for work and Caroline called me at night to speak to Sacha as she was behaving badly, and Caroline was unable to control her. Sacha said that she went to bed at the same time as her mother, but that Caroline was making her do everything. All the tidying up and housework.

Sacha said that Caroline was still in bed at 8am yesterday and she had to get Alice ready for school. See what happens when I'm away.

November 11th 2013 20.00

Tonight, she started shouting at me for coming in the double doors.

Then she shouted at Alice for bringing a Lego toy downstairs.

Then she went mad at the cat because it wanted food when she was getting the washing out of the machine.

Then she started shouting at Sacha telling her not to come downstairs after her bath and she won't get any supper and then shouted at her to say not to ask about having any friends around after school again.

November 13th 2013 00.00 Midnight

I just got out of the bath and was brushing my teeth when Caroline came up to me and started shouting at me saying that I had made her bedtime cup of tea too late and that I shouldn't have bothered or should have done it earlier. Very ungrateful.

Then when I came to bed 5 minutes later she started shouting at me saying the same thing again that she had just shouted at me earlier. Then she said I had done nothing all evening apart from some ironing (about 1 ½ hrs. actually) and that I'd been home all day and had done nothing at all in the house. No mention or understanding that the fact was that I was actually working from home and had lots of work to do.

She said she was fed up tidying the house on a Saturday after I make a mess on a Friday and that I should tidy it up on a Friday even though I am out at work. Duh, how can I tidy the house when I'm not there?

I shouted at her to shut up, but she just went on and on and on like she always does nah nah nah nah nah nah on and on and on pushing and pushing me until I lose my temper as I can't stand it any longer.

In the end I got up and punched the wardrobe door and knocked her make-up and rubbish onto the floor and then went to the spare room again.

She is so horrible to me, she never appreciates anything I do when all she does is sit on the sofa with the laptop wedged on her fat stomach tapping away and stuffing her face with crap getting fatter and fatter. Then eventually at about midnight she gets up and starts shouting and having a go at me for bugger all or just the slightest thing in her head. The pattern is repeated over and over, just the circumstances vary slightly.

My life is a f***ing misery. How can I get away from this nasty bitch that treats me like shit???!!!

November 13th 2013 12.20pm

She started shouting at me and telling me to wash my hands because I had picked up the doormat to shake it out the door. Another new OCD rule.

I was defiant as this was just another rubbish stupid rule and so when I refused she started hitting me in the chest punching and grabbing me. I tried to grab her to stop her and she screamed like a mad woman and said she'd call the police. All I was doing was trying to stop her attacking me.

When I let go of her she started hitting me again, but I moved away to another room and shut the door and held it closed so she couldn't get at me.

This was absolutely OTT and she then carried on shouting at me through the door that the house is a mess and that it is all because I made it a mess yesterday and it's all my fault and that I am totally useless.

Then she told me to leave her. To move out and then she would stop working and I'd have to pay for everything. More emotional blackmail.

I feel so trapped and abused by this mental case who is supposed to be my wife. I have thought about leaving but I am really worried if I do leave that she will not be able to cope and will harm the children even more than what happens when I am there. I need to protect them.

November 14th 2013 08.50

She started shouting at me because I didn't start looking at her pension documents the exact second she asked me to do so because I was in the middle of serving breakfast to the kids.

Then she went on at me saying that I didn't have a pension at the moment and saying that I was thick, stupid and that our children get their intelligence from her not me.

Then she carried on having a go at me for using the wrong porridge oats to make her breakfast, which wasn't even true. She then spent another 20 minutes slagging me off and being nasty to me. Par for the course really.

November 15th 2013 21.00

Tonight, I got home late because I was stuck for over two hours in a traffic jam on the A1.

When I got in Caroline was in such an awful mood and she just went to bed so I went and slept in the spare room again. Peace and quiet.

November 15th 2013 22.00

Caroline has been drinking a lot recently. She has drunk almost a bottle of Vodka in less than a week plus she is eating loads of chocolate and crisps. Sacha says she ate all of hers and Alice's Halloween sweets! She stole the kid's sweets.

November 16th 2013 18.55

Tonight has been a complete and utter nightmare.

She rang me at work in the morning asking me to go to Asda to buy some washing liquid and other bits because she couldn't be bothered going out to the supermarket. She used those exact words. She could not be bothered going 5 minutes away to the local supermarket.

So I did, which meant I got home at 6.50pm about 35 minutes later than normal as you might expect having gone to a supermarket when asked.

The minute I walked in the door she started shouting at me for being late again and that I'd be late tomorrow and that this job was no better and I had to take Alice upstairs and read her a book right now.

I went to move the cars around ready for the next day and when I came back in she started on at me again shouting and swearing at me. I shouted back and swore back at her giving her the same.

Then when I went upstairs I heard Alice, who was also upstairs, shouting down at her to 'shut up' and stop shouting at Daddy. She then came running upstairs shouting at Alice and she shouted back at her saying "F*** off Mummy" several times.

Sacha was also upstairs and laughed at this. Caroline went mad and chased Sacha to her room, kicked over her toy boat and then hit her on the back and shoulder leaving nail marks and a red slap mark in the middle of her back. Sacha was almost naked as she had just come out of the bath a minute before.

I ran over to help Sacha and had to physically haul Caroline away. I pushed and pulled Caroline off Sacha and out of the way sending her out of Sacha's bedroom.

I really thought Caroline was going to turn and start hitting me right then but this time for some reason she didn't. I told her to get away and stop hitting our children. I then told her I'd leave her if she ever hit either of our children again.

I told her to get away from us all and leave us alone, but she carried on shouting at us all. I tried to hold the bedroom door closed so that she would stay away from the kids, but she yanked it open cutting my arm in the process on the door frame.

After some more shouting she eventually stopped and went into the bedroom and just had a shower whilst I read to Alice to calm and reassure her.

I then did my usual routine of clearing up the kitchen, making lunches and spent a bit of time with Sacha trying to comfort her and help her out.

I was remarkably calm through all this and think it was lucky that she didn't hit me or Alice this time, but she was so out of order and out of control it was frightening for me let alone the kids.

I was really scared for the kids and they should not have to endure this. She needs help but won't face up to it - she says it is always me, it's always my fault. OK yes, I don't often handle it well, but she always starts it and goes on and on and on winding me up till I can't take it any longer. Pushing my buttons and egging me on until I shout back at her.

I've tried ignoring her and walking away but she carries on, follows me and gets nasty and personal saying horrible things about me and my family and our friends. She often insults my mum who she calls a poison dwarf or attacks me by saying I've got a tiny penis or that I am thick or a short-arsed idiot.

I've tried so many things to not react or to deal with her outbursts. Such as covering my ears to drown her out but if I do that she says that I am a mental case when I do it and that mental health issues run in my family because my Aunty had a breakdown and was crazy. I can't win no matter what I try to do.

This has been going on for years – I have tried to explain to so many people at my various workplaces and they have known she was mad, but no-one really knows the reality and the full extent of it all and I doubt anybody would believe me in any case. It's too crazy to comprehend. How can a grown man just accept such bad behaviour, verbal and physical abuse as well as all the emotional and mental stuff?

I only wish I started recording it sooner.

How can I get us out of this?!! Do I call social services? Then what can I do as I can't look after the kid's full time and work full time as I do now? Trapped in a living hell! That's what it feels like!

I have no friends anymore that I can turn to. I talk to some people at my work, but they are not near me and not that close that I would call for help or real support. My parents are miles away and years ago I told them not to interfere in my marriage. They know what she is like but it's too far down the line. I have nowhere to go and nowhere to turn, I feel so isolated.

November 17th 2013 21.30

I arrived home late again due to an accident on the motorway. When I got in she just stared at me and scowled at me and then went to bed and didn't speak to me at all for the whole night.

Another night with no tea! I will have to just make something myself but at least I have some peace and quiet. Can't she understand that when I have to drive 2 ½ hours to London for work in the morning and then at least the same back I am tired and at times traffic will delay the journey. Why is she so mean and self-centred? I hate coming home.

November 18th 2013 07.50

As usual I made Caroline her lunch for work, egg sandwiches, and put them in her handbag but she just took them out and put them in the fridge.

So then I took them to work so they weren't wasted and ate them myself. How petty and childish.

November 19th 2013 07.10

I'm driving to work, and she called me on the phone and just shouted at me for not cleaning the hob and for not emptying the dishwasher in the kitchen. Nice. She broke her silence.

November 20th 2013 00.30 midnight

We had a fairly pleasant evening and watched The Apprentice together. Our first evening spending some time together for a long time. Sometimes things can be ok, but it always seems to lull me into a false sense of hope.

I then went for a bath at 11.30 and when I came down afterwards I said, "come on it's time for bed" and she just shouted at me saying why am I saying that?

Then she said, "make me a cup of tea" (this is way after midnight and I've been up since 6) but not in a nice way at all. It was really more of an order than any type of request.

So, I made her a cup of tea like a dutiful husband, but she complained about it and shouted at me again. This time because I had not brewed it long enough she told me to do another one and leave the teabag in, so I did and went to bed in the spare room again.

She had spent almost all the evening as usual parked in her spot lying on the sofa with her laptop on her belly eating crap and drunk about 4 Vodkas.

November 25th 2013 17.45

Came home to Caroline shouting at Sacha about homework and school test results. It was not nice at all and very unfair what she was saying. Poor girl but lucky she stopped right after I came home.

December

December 2nd 2013 16.00

Again, she rang me up at work and started shouting at me, this time because I had not cleared away all the breakfast porridge bowls - here we go again. The calm periods seem to be getting less and less. She is building up and I am sure it's pretty soon going to blow up again.

December 2nd 2013 18.00

She rang me up again when I was in the car driving from work and started shouting at me because I had not cleared away all the breakfast porridge bowls again.

When I got home that evening at 7pm after being stuck in a jam on A1 the kids were just having tea all because she spent half an hour clearing up breakfast things?! It makes no sense and she just uses anything she can to have a go at me.

December 3rd 2013 00.10 am

Caroline woke me up when I was sleeping and told me to get up as she felt sick??!! She wasn't sick, and I have no idea why I was supposed to get up.

December 5th 2013 02.40 am

Caroline, for some reason, was still awake reading and not talking to me. Sometimes she does this. When she is brewing or concocting something she can't sleep and mulls it all over and over keeping me awake and deliberately disturbing me. Often, she will wake me up to have a go. I'm waiting for it.

December 7th 2013 18.25

Came in from work to a complete mess and all were just finishing drinking their tea.

She told me I couldn't go out (I was due to meet a couple of friends for a curry) because the place was a mess and I needed to clean up, do lunches, empty bins, put Alice to bed, empty the washing machine, write Christmas cards, create a letter for my friends and do a title page for Sacha's homework.

Meanwhile she sat on her fat arse again saying she hadn't stopped all day. Not stopped doing what? The place was a real mess.

There was no tea for me and she complained when I got a pizza out of the freezer and cooked it in the oven for myself.

Then she moaned at me for about an hour going on about how she organises everything and I do nothing telling me to sort out my grandads presents myself etc. and buy my own meals and organise them myself for tea etc., going on and on.

Not allowing me to go out with my friends from work, this is controlling me. I never go out and the one time I plan – with her prior permission, she throws a fit and stops me all because it means she has to do something and can't just sit doing nothing all night.

December 11ᵗʰ 2013 09.00

I asked when we were going to collect orders from butchers at Christmas and she went mad shouting at me that I had to do it on Christmas eve and that it was all I did at Christmas and my bloody work should not get in the way, that I had to collect at 6am and then go in to work after. I'd planned to go in at 4 or 5am because we had so much work on getting the Boxing Day sale ready.

Then went on a tirade about my work and it was taking over our lives and no better than last job etc. etc. Again, out of order and totally unfounded. I took this job closer to home in Leeds, so I was not away 2-3 nights a week like before.

December 12ᵗʰ 2013 08.30

Caroline went mad at me whilst I was cleaning the oven as she could see a few drops of water on the floor and going mental about chemicals in the cleaning stuff - way OTT. It was only a few drips and easily cleaned up. No need for such a fuss.

December 14th 2013 08.10

Caroline rang me up at work to complain that I hadn't emptied the dishwasher again last night when I had been downstairs on my own after she went to bed for an additional 3 hours. A slight exaggeration and of course no recognition of the other stuff I did do to tidy up. She expects just to go to bed and leave me to tidy everything up on my own before I can go to bed – even any mess she has made. Ridiculous.

December 14th 2013 16.25

She rang me up again while I was at work to see if I had left work yet and shouted at me when I said I hadn't. The thing is, we didn't arrange for me to leave work early. I can't just leave early anytime I like but in this instance, I had to leave immediately and drive back home to make tea for everyone.

December 15th 2013 22.00

It has been pretty quiet today for a change but only as she is ill and in bed. However, she still managed to shout at me a few times. Can you believe it?

December 15th 2013 23.00

I went to go to bed but then she started shouting at me about sausages that I somehow had to prepare as she was too ill to get them out the packet. What on earth was she talking about and where did this all come from? I have no idea. She also said that I needed to be home from work at 5pm to give the kids tea which would mean leaving work early again.

So, I decided to go to bed in the spare room on my own again.

December 16th 2013 00.05am

She came into my room, the spare room, and was shouting at me calling me a 'f***ing bastard' and saying I was always useless when she was ill and what would I be like with her when she was old?

Then she went downstairs for a drink or something – and when she came back up she came back to my room, threw open the door and put on the light for no reason other than to be nasty and wake me up and disturb me.

After that outburst and crazy behaviour, I just couldn't get to sleep as I was wondering what she was going to do next. I was thinking that perhaps she would come back and start hitting me or something like that. It would not have been the first time. She seems to prey at night when I am tired, and I need sleep.

There is definitely something seriously wrong with that woman. She needs help and not from me.

December 16th 2013 17.30

She rang me on my mobile whilst I was working to find out why I wasn't home yet and shouted at me yelling me she was ill, and I should be home early. But when we spoke earlier at around 4pm she said she was fine and that it was ok for me not to leave early and come back a bit later. As I had left early other nights, I was topping to make sure I did some extra and not get into trouble.

December 17th 2013 00.05am

I decided to bite the bullet and finally go in the bed with her in our room, but she just started having a go at me about my job, that it was terrible and that I have done nothing at all the whole week in the house and that I contributed nothing to the house and home.

She called my boss a stupid cow and told me to tell her not to call me outside of work and that I should get her to do the Saturday night reports for work. Caroline was demanding to know exactly what my boss had said about my early leaving on Fridays and childcare. She was going on and on and on, so I went back to my room again. It's no longer the spare room, but my room now.

She is a bitch - a fat bitch!

December 17th 2013 23.00

Caroline just went mad at me because she had asked me to get some shower gel and I thought she meant a hand wash, so I brought the wrong thing to her in the bathroom. It was a simple error and nothing that deserves the berating she was giving me.

When I came back with a shower gel she just kept on shouting at me and didn't take it from me when I held it out, so I just dropped it on the floor. That's when she started screaming at me which went on for absolutely ages.

Then I washed my hands and she started screaming at me because her shower went cold. Aha – revenge is sweet!

After that she carried on shouting at me about any old rubbish she could think of for about 20 minutes until she seemed to run out of abuse to hurl at me.

She is definitely 100% a nutcase.

December 18th 2013 10.00

She lost her temper with Alice simply because she wiped her nose on the bedding. As she was manhandling and dragging her out of her bedroom she was shouting at her and then she hurt her toes on the door. Out of order against the poor little sweetheart.

December 18th 2013 11.00

She just went completely mental and screaming at me because the hoover caught her back as she went past me when I was hoovering the stairs. It was her own fault. She was screaming at me and slamming doors.

I was certain she was building up to the point where she'll hit me later. I can just see it coming.

December 23rd 2013 20.10

This one was not mad like usual - just weird!

I arrived home with her mum at 8pm as I was bringing over from London to spend Christmas with us. Caroline was already in bed at that time (because she still has a cold after over a week and was still so ill). Now bear in mind the fact that she has not seen her mother at all since early October. Well she didn't even attempt to get out of bed to say hello or greet her in any way at all. She just stayed there, in bed in her room on her computer and watching TV. Now that is not normal is it?

December 27th 2013 22.00

After a pretty surprising and nice Christmas, where Caroline has been on her completely best behaviour, the spell was broken. Tonight, she started shouting at me because she wanted to resend an email and couldn't do it. I said to her to just forward the email but somehow when she did that it lost the email address.

Instead of trying to do undo or fix it she just started shouting and stormed off upstairs. When she came out the shower she started shouting at me again about the fact I was looking at iTunes apps for Sacha and I should look at them on her laptop, but I'd closed it down. So, she went mad at me again saying it was the third time she'd looked at apps and I was never going to download them and what had I been doing all night? Bla bla bla the usual rubbish.

December 31st 2013 01.10pm

She started having a go at me because I touched the bath mat and then flushed the toilet. She made me go and get an antibacterial wipe to clean it.

January

January 5th 2014 05.10

I was away with work and she rang me up at 05.10 in the morning because Alice had been keeping her up all night, like it was my fault.

She said she hated her and he was ruining her life and that she was worried she was going to hit her.

She rang me again to get me to tell her to go to bed to sleep which of course I did.

She then told me she thinks there is something wrong with her, that she is a crazy girl. What an awful way to talk about your daughter.

She then told me that I couldn't ever be away again for work and that I must tell that effing woman, my boss that if she wanted someone in London that she should get someone else as I was not prepared to do it again.

She then started having a go at me blaming me for everything and all about my job and everything else she was unhappy about, so I hung up. Her attitude about Alice was terrible.

She said she had been shouting at her which would not have helped. No wonder he wasn't sleeping and playing up. You can't shout at a young child in such a vicious manner and not expect it to have some negative impact.

She told me he had weed on her bed at around midnight so no doubt she shouted at her which upset her and set her off on her bad behaviour. It's her own fault, not her.

Also, she ought to have considered that I was away, and I had been with her all day every day for a whole week prior to that so he was missing me and unsettled.

I feel terrible for her, my poor little girl who is upset, unsettled and missing me and it looks like Caroline just can't handle her. He needs love and understanding not insults and abuse.

Also, it now looks like the pre- menstrual black zone is being entered once again.

January 9th 2014 12.00pm

She was going on and on at Sacha about her comprehension work saying the work she had done was rubbish and that Sacha was either lazy or stupid. An awful way to handle it.

Then she pushed Sacha who fell to the floor. Totally out of order and unnecessary. Then she was being mean and horrible to Sacha and constantly nagging and shouting at her, being totally mean for hours.

January 11th 2014 19.25

She, the crazy one, rang me up again whilst I was in the car driving on my way home and shouted "where the f*** are you" when I answered.

So, when I told her where I was on the A1 which was still about 45 minutes away she went mad at me because she couldn't cope with Alice and she desperately wanted me home to deal with her. She also said that I was to tell that f***ing woman (referring to my boss) that I wasn't working in London anymore and I had to always be home at a decent time.

So, I hung up on her as I had no intention of listening to more of her rubbish.

She bares no acknowledgement that I have a job and I need to work. Yes, my boss is also a crazy nut job, but she is my boss. Or even that sometimes my work and my team need me to be there for them and so things and that sometimes driving that distance can be fraught with problems and delays. It's always all about her. Me, me, me and how things affect her and cause her extra work. Except it's not extra work its normal family stuff that a mother and wife should be doing.

January 11th 2014 21.00

She started shouting at me the second she came off the phone after talking with her mum. It was all about me putting the washing away, about the dishwasher, about the fact the house was seemingly, in her opinion of course, a complete mess. Then that I had loads to do and asking me why had I sat down and not completed all my tasks? Saying again that my job was complete

89

shit and she wouldn't allow me to work late anymore and saying that she couldn't cope with Alice etc...

Completely out of order, irrational and unfair as always.

No doubt she will hit me soon again – the mental phase of the loony cycle has definitely started.

January 25th 2014 19.00

This evening I was shouted at for taking too long eating my evening meal. Really? There is a time limit set for eating food or is it a speed enforcement order or something?

This then turned into another 30-minute tirade about me always leaving her to do everything and never doing anything and about me coming in late from work at 6.35pm tonight. The normal journey from my office takes just over an hour if I drive like an idiot so getting in at 6.35pm isn't really late is it?

February

February 4th 2014 18.50

It has started again.

She came in the door from work and started shouting at me because there were shoes on the mat by the door. Then she started shouting at Sacha because she took too long coming out of the swimming pool.

Then she started wiping all the food from Aldi with antibacterial wipes, this is a new one with her OCD rubbish. Now we have to wipe all food we buy from the supermarket with antibacterial wipes before it is put away in the cupboards. After that she started shouting at me and telling me that I had to put all the food stuff away and wipe it as I did it.

Then I asked her to stop shouting and swearing at me, so she hit me 3 times punching me with full force on the chest, proper punches. Then she carried on shouting for about a further 10 minutes and also started shouting at Sacha.

She was shouting once again about my job. Saying that it was as shit as the last one I had, the one I changed from to not work away all the time. Then saying it was all my fault that I lost my job before, which was a really good one and close to home. It's always a blame game with her blaming someone else, normally me for whatever she is unhappy about. I never lost any job, I was made redundant by the bank I worked at.

She was then shouting and again saying that I never did anything round the house it was all down to her to do everything and that I never did any shopping etc. etc.

She was acting like a complete and utter lunatic, so it looks like I am going to have a great day off tomorrow.

February 5th 2014 17.10

Saturday morning and she started the day by shouting at me because the house was a mess like it was my fault.

Then for no reason she was criticising me for the way I was cooking the risotto for tea and then going on at me about the clothes washing and general bla bla bla, the usual rubbish ranting that she does. I pretty much just switched off and smiled at her while she poured out her tirade of abuse and rubbish. If I was to believe all she ever said about me I'd be just a docile quivering wreck. It's so bad.

February 9th 2014 21.00

Caroline started by nagging me about the fact that earlier I had leant into her car to get a school form out of it. All I did was lean into the car.

She was going on asking "did I touch or lean on anything with my coat"? Telling me to take it off and put it away from all my other coats as the car is dirty. This is all because she used that car for work, so it is dirty and full of germs. I don't know anyone in their right mind that has two cars, one for work and one for normal use? This is OCD way over the top and all totally in her head, yet we must do all she says. Paranoid crazy or what?

Then later she started moaning at me because I was getting my clothes out and ready for work tomorrow. Apparently now I have to get 5 sets out on a Sunday for the whole week and put them in the back bedroom??!! What is that about?

February 11th 2014 17.30

She rang me when she left work - I put the phone on speaker as I was making kids tea and needed my hands free.

She then started moaning that she couldn't hear me properly, so I raised my voice, so she could but then she said "f*** off" and put the phone down on me.

February 12th 2014 14.00

I came in from taking Sacha to spend some time playing at one of her friend's house. This is the only way she can get to play with her friends as she won't ever let us bring any people to our house at all now. Then she started shouting at me for putting something down on the stairs – another new rule.

Then she spent half an hour going on at me and shouting about housework, paperwork, the whole house being a mess, that she does everything, and I do nothing. Her same old ranting rubbish. Getting a bit boring, can't she find something new to shout at me about?

February 12th 2014 17.10

The Dragon started shouting at me because I had bought full fat coconut milk. Seemingly the fat cow is now on a diet but never told me so how would I know?

She went on at me for half an hour about there being no food in the house, that I was disorganised and did nothing. That she did everything in the house and the house was a mess yesterday all because she didn't tidy up. Telling me I now needed to go out to the supermarket shopping at 8pm at night and then just more ranting rubbish until I just couldn't take it any longer and so I stormed off to get away from her.

She is treating me like I'm some sort of kid or imbecile. She is a horrible cow and I hate her fat guts.

I am trapped in a f***ing nightmare between work shit and this shit. I don't know how long I can take it all. I can't see a way out of this misery at all though. She will start shouting at me again as whilst I am doing this, recording these notes in my phone, I should be cooking tea. I'm so sure she will start hitting me again soon. I just learned that she has her period - wow that's a surprise!!?

February 13th 2014 10.00

She started shouting at me to hurry up as she had to go and then going on at me because Sacha had lost her play script for school. Then shouting because she had no lunch ready and made for her by me for work.

Then she left and came back as she forgot tampons. She sent me to go upstairs and get them but shouted at me because I didn't get them quick enough.

February 20th 2014 18.50

Tonight, it's my birthday so you would expect a good night except history tells me it won't be. Low and behold she was giving Alice a bath but didn't wipe her bum properly after going to the toilet and some poo went in the bath. She went crazy at her and I was called to deal with it and clean the bath.

Whilst I was in the kitchen and before I could get up there I heard her shout at Alice and then heard a big slap sound as she hit her.

When I got there, I found that she had slapped her on the back and given her a big red hand mark on her back which obviously hurt her a lot and the poor sweetheart was crying (I took a photo of it).

I shouted at her not to hit her. Then she shouted at me for telling her not to hit her and then stormed off and slammed the door to her room. Some birthday this is but I expected nothing less.

When I think about it she always makes a fuss on my birthday or Father's Day. It's like she can't handle the attention and focus on someone else and she does whatever she can to draw it back to herself. This woman has some real problems and there is no way I'm able to fix any of it especially when she won't even acknowledge there is a problem.

February 21st 2014 09.00

She rang me up while I was at work to have a moan at me because Sacha had put her red coat on top of some other coats on the hanger. What could possibly be wrong with that I hear you say? Well seemingly she had worn it when she was out at the doctors the other week. Therefore, it is 'infected' with doctor's surgery germs which are along with hospitals the worst kind. The coat needs to be washed before it can be used again and now all the other coats it has touched and 'infected' also need to be washed. Who even washes coats and jackets?

So just because a coat was worn at the doctors a few weeks ago all the coats need to be washed? Weird or what? This is more than just some OCD issue it's far worse. I made no fuss and got on with it. Anything for peace and quiet.

Although that is part of the problem. If we don't pander to all the weird and stupid demands she goes crazy. So, we do follow them, and it seems to feed her OCD. If we go along with the rules she seems to make up more. Maybe it's all designed for us to not follow the rules, so she can blame us and explode and provoke us. When we do follow them she is still frustrated and unhappy, maybe that's it? She is never happy, never satisfied with anything anyway.

February 26th 2014 08.40

The Dragon got up at 8.40am and just started shouting at me asking what the hell had I been doing all morning since getting up earlier as the whole place was a complete mess?

In fact, I had been preparing the packed lunch for us going on a day trip out to Hadrian's Wall, getting Alice's breakfast for her and put in a load of washing so it wasn't like I hadn't done anything. It was because I hadn't done exactly what it was in her head that she wanted me to do.

February 27th 2014 12.00pm

She has been mad from the minute she got up this morning and all because we have some visitors coming to the house. These are not just any visitors but our best friends Greg and Sally who have been to our house so many times before but not so much recently because of the OCD issues.

She was rabbiting on and on about things not being all tidy and all clean. She was acting pure mental and telling me to do this, that and the next thing in the most horrible manner.

She was shouting at me again when I was preparing the chicken for lunch. Nagging at me to wash my hands all the time and not to touch anything at all due to chicken germ contamination. In her mind raw chicken is completely covered in salmonella and its spread all over just by looking at the bloody chicken. So, if any raw chicken is being handled then she goes so far over the top, it's unbelievable. Normally I make sure she can't see me doing it, isn't aware or do it well in advance when she is out. The stress and reaction from her is just too much.

Then a short while later she screamed in Sacha's face because she didn't give her the sky remote immediately upon her demanding it from her. I don't seem to know or identify any difference now between then pre-menstrual Caroline and the non-menstrual Caroline any more......??!!

March

March 1ˢᵗ 2014 23.00

She started shouting at me because I had gone upstairs and
fallen asleep. I had gone up to bed and laid down and just
dropped off straight away as I was so tired.

She started shouting at me and telling me I had to go
downstairs and tidy up all the mess that was down there.
Mostly mess of her doing.

March 10ᵗʰ 2014 18.40-21.40

She has been moaning, shouting and nagging at me for hours
tonight. It started the minute I walked through the door after
work. She was shouting about anything and everything as usual
and to be honest I just totally switched off and let the rubbish
just wash over my head.

She is completely mad, and her behaviour is so out of order. Its
bloody mental torture.

March 11ᵗʰ 2014 21.00

Not too bad so far today, got off lightly but guess what? Oh no
The Grouch's period started last night so she is going to get
worse for sure.

March 15ᵗʰ 2014 17.45

I came home to find her being a complete mental case. She had
one of Alice's friends round to play after school and this boy
tramped through the house with his outdoor shoes on. This
meant that I had to mop the whole of the downstairs floor using
a bleach concentrate as soon as the boy had been collected by
his mother.

Whilst I was doing it the kids were playing in the living room.
Caroline went in and started screaming at them both because
they were playing football. She then proceeded to hit both
Sacha and Alice which was way out of order and uncalled for.
She is getting more and more out of control and I am so worried
that it's going to escalate one time. I don't know how long I can
continue to keep my cool for.

March 18th 2014 19.30

She came home really late from work having gone to Aldi to buy some shopping. She never told me she was doing that, so I had no idea where she was. Who can take two hours to shop at Aldi? It's the smallest supermarket ever.

She then parked her car in the middle of the drive sticking miles out and blocking all other cars in. I hate it when she does this because it's a real pain to get my car out and I'm not allowed to touch or go into her infected work car. So, I asked her to move it and park it properly.

Well you can guess what happened. She went mental at me, shouting and screaming in my face about how she was really tired and had no time for any lunch at work and was at work till 6pm because she was so busy. Now isn't this the person who has no understanding of why sometimes I leave work late? Double standards.

She went back out in the end and actually moved the car but only about 2ft which was not enough. She then got the door stuck open on the trellis fence and came back in the house screaming at me, so I went out myself and parked it properly. A big mistake.

She came out with her coat on and was shouting at me outside the house on the driveway and then she threw the set of car keys at me hitting me right in the balls. Pretty good shot really but it damn hurt me.

Then after I moved the car and went back inside she carried on screaming at me for about half an hour telling me to sort out the shopping etc. This was not just shouting but full on banshee screaming fit.

Later, because I had not cooked her tea and I had not yet eaten as I was waiting for her, she went mad again throwing open the door to the room and yelling at me about how she had no tea.

So, I cooked tea for us both but she stayed upstairs and so I slept in the spare room, my room, again.

March 19th 2014 12.00pm

I came back from Alice's swimming and ballet with her to find her being mean to Sacha and making Sacha do a load of housework. Sacha said she had pulled her hair and screamed in her face.

I confronted Caroline about this, but she denied it and she said all she'd done was pull her hair and shout at her a little bit.

Then she turned on me and started saying Sacha was lazy and good for nothing just like me and a load of other stuff just like that.

I walked away from her and went upstairs to find Sacha and comfort her.

A fat horrible cow and an unfit mother that's what she is.

March 23rd 2014 20.00

She spent almost all the evening moaning and nagging me for anything and everything. She was shouting and swearing at me for absolutely nothing. About how I was doing the clearing up, about the way I was cooking tea and then about not cooking tea etc.

March 24th 2014 18.30

She rang me only to shout at me for not emptying the dishwasher.

March 24th 2014 19.30

She started by moaning at me about dishwasher again.

After I had been out I came back home and then I walked into the utility room and she was behind the door, but I had no idea. So, then she went mental at me all because the coats that were hung up on the back of the door had touched her. I didn't know she was in there, Alice was in the bath and I heard her talking so thought that she was upstairs with her. However, she was actually downstairs in the utility room feeding the cat. Then as per usual she went on at me for so many silly things such as the fact I was wearing the same top that I had just worn in the car picking up Sacha.

So, she then took the cup of tea that she had made for me and poured it away in spite. She continued to shout at me to get myself on with doing all my jobs and that I couldn't stop until every single one was completed. Then she moaned at me for touching sausages and nagged at me to disinfect the worktop down. After that she was having a right go at me for filling the kettle with water?!

This continued with her complaining and shouting at me for the temperature I was cooking the sausages at and the fact the rice was on too high a heat on the hob and might boil over. Shouting at me because Alice had lost her bunny which was her favourite toy and always sleeps with it and then because I wore my slippers in the bedroom.

April

April 5th 2014 21.00

She was just awful and moaning about everything bla bla bla.

April 10th 2014

Caroline's period started – fun time begins.

April 17th 2014 19.00

We came back from staying away at my parents in Wales and she was crazy. Everything had to be wiped with anti-bacterial wipes; all bags and contents. The Children had to stay outside the house and then head straight into the bath once they went inside. This is because we were all contaminated due to being at my parents' house. It seems their house is al contaminated with germs and we are all going to die.

This is so completely mad and irrational. It's her OCD and all in her head. If we breach any of her made up rules in the slightest then we are in massive trouble and get shouted or screamed at maybe even hit.

Then she was also saying some horrible and nasty things about my parents. She does this a lot. Calling my mum a poison dwarf and a weak doormat for my father. Saying she just panders to my dad all the time. She also says that my dad is a horrible bully and bullies my mum. All this is supposed to antagonise me and get a reaction. Sometimes if I don't react she just keeps going and steps it all up to another level and sometimes she just gives up and goes away. This time she went away.

April 25th 2014 22.00

At 10pm tonight she finally got off her fat arse and realised that things needed sorting for the kids going back to school tomorrow so the inevitable happened and she started shouting at me and Sacha about her PE kit etc.

In the playroom Sacha was going to put some photos in her bag and Caroline started screaming in her face to go to bed and grabbed her arm hurting her.

After that I endured about half an hour of her madness, shouting and swearing at me before she went for a shower and then bed.

April 27th 2014 07.30

Caroline fell over and cut her knee whilst chasing Sacha to hit her, serves her right. Sacha says that Caroline slapped her on the bum and in the face. I didn't see it happen but can totally believe it.

April 27th 2014 21.00

She started shouting at me for the way that I sprayed the worktop with antibacterial spray. It seems that the way I sprayed it meant that it would spray around but isn't that the whole idea of a spray?

She then launched into her usual tirade of abuse at me about my family and me. Insulting me and them for about half an hour. Then she went upstairs and came back down nice as pie for a whole 5 minutes and then started all over again. This happened about 3 times over the next hour and was just like some sort of split personality schizophrenic.

April 29th 2014 01.00

At about 1am in the morning Caroline came into the back bedroom, my bedroom, where I was already fast asleep and started shouting at me waking me up in the process.

She was shouting and saying why didn't I tell her I was going to bed and that she thought I was watching a film downstairs or something and she was waiting up for me.

May

May 2nd 2014 11.30am

Firstly, a short while earlier she was shouting at Alice because as she says she was being 'stupid' which means she was just being a typical little girl. She shouted at her and said, "shut up you cheeky little twat". Then she made me put her in her room.

Caroline went mental screaming at Sacha because her English Sat's work was not good enough and she wasn't happy with it. She always has exacting standards and when things don't meet them she loses it.

Caroline screamed in Sacha's face and then slapped her on the back. The slap was so hard I could hear it where I was all the way upstairs.

Then Caroline went into Sacha's room and started shouting at her all because her room was a mess and telling her to clean it and dust it. She was screaming and shouting in her face in the most aggressive and horrible way.

I am certain that she would have hit Sacha again had I not stepped in to stop her. I had to physically put myself between Caroline and Sacha, so she could not reach her.

She is absolutely mental and out of control.

Days off here at home with her are awful - we all love our Sundays when she is at work and we have peace, quiet and plenty of fun.

May 5th 2014 20.00

She called me when I was again driving home in the car shouting at me about being late home on a Thursday.

May 5th 2014 21.00

When I got home, Sacha told me that Caroline stood on her foot and when Sacha shouted "ow" because it hurt Caroline told her to f*** off.

Sacha says that Caroline has been horrible all evening to her and Alice.

May 6th 2014 20.00

Sacha told me that Caroline hit her twice this morning. The first time was when she was eating her breakfast and the second time was when she was brushing her teeth with no apparent reason for either attack.

Sacha said she also screamed right in her face several times repeating the same thing just like she does to me. It seems I cannot leave her to look after the children.

May 9th 2014 06.30

As soon as Caroline got up she started having a go at me simply because I had gotten up early to go for a run. She said I was disturbing Sacha as she needed extra sleep for her SATS.

She was being unreasonable, out of order and downright nasty.

May 12th 2014 23.50

I was asleep in bed and she started shouting at me and waking me up to tell me to go downstairs and empty the washing machine. The washing that she forgot to empty but saying it was my fault that she forgot to empty it and I should have done it anyway. So, I got up and did it. What a fool.

Whilst I was putting the washing out on the clothes dryer she started shouting at me about her phone cord being tangled up with her hair dryer cord. She was saying that I tangled it all up and I have no idea how?

It is now past midnight and I need to be up at 4.20am to drive up to London for work - so nice.

May 14th 2014 08.00

Caroline rang me twice whilst I was at work with Alice screaming in the background. She was saying that she woke her up and that she was a 'little shit'.

She cannot control her at all and when he starts or even just needs something she handles it so badly that all she does is to get mad at her, shout at her and wind her up and upset her even more.

I'm so worried she'll hit her again, but I am 200 miles away.

What happened was that Alice was bouncing a bouncy ball in the hallway when it went onto the doormat inside the front door. She just went on the mat to get it like any normal person would, but this is against the rules. The mat is the transition between the outside and germs and the inside and safety. Her reaction was predictable, she went mad, shouted at her and then picked her up holding her in the air.

She then shouted for me to come and wipe her feet to clean them and then sat her on the sofa and shouted at her not to move a single muscle. Before I could get there, she put her foot down on the carpet and then she went totally mental. She screamed at her and smacked her so hard that Sacha could hear it from her room upstairs.

It all happened so fast I couldn't get there in time to stop it. She was over the top and way out of order. She hurt my poor little girl and there was nothing I could do. It was done before I got there. I shouted at her to get out, to get away from her and leave us. I told her never to touch her again. I thought she was going to start on me. I wanted her to because I was at that point not going to hold back but she just stared at me for a few seconds and then walked away. I so wanted to just lay her out there and then and be done with it, be done with her but again I didn't. It's not me to do that but then I can't stand back and let this carry on any longer except I have no idea where to turn or what to do.

May 18th 2014 20.00

I came home at 6.30pm after picking up Sacha from tennis club and I then had to make tea as the kids had had no food yet despite her being at home all day.

May 20th 2014 18.30

Caroline had been ok and calm so far again today, but it could not last the whole day. When I came in after being outside playing with Alice I found out that she had screamed at Sacha and hit her again.

This was seemingly because Sacha was saying something, some problem with her phone and Caroline was busy. She was just in the middle of her OCD crazy wiping of all the shopping from Aldi with antibacterial wipes as it is all 'dirty and infected' with germs. Nothing important except in her mad OCD brain and no justification for anything.

May 26th 2014 07.00

She started shouting at me for the way I was unloading the dishwasher. I was doing it all wrong and not the way she demands it. I just ignored her and carried on doing it the way I was doing it. She glared at me and stormed off.

May 31st 2014 19.00

Caroline ordered Sacha to put away her own clothes washing but when Sacha refused she screamed at her and hit her on her head and then she threw the washing at her.

When I defended Sacha and stood up for her Caroline then as per normal form started on me. She was shouting at me and insulting my family again. Saying they were tight, slagging off my parents, my uncle Ronnie and my brother as well. It was all just nasty. Then she went back to Sacha saying she was lazy and useless etc...

June

June 1st 2014 17.00

Today she has been completely mental.

She was moaning the whole time we were in Harrogate about how she didn't want to go there because she worked there all the time anyway and because it is all dirty and full of scummy people.

Also moaning about the way I was driving. Saying it was too slow, then it was too fast and then she started slagging off my family once more.

Later after Alice had been at the doctors with me for her jab she went mad, mad, mad. She had to have a bath and so did I. Then we had to change all our clothes due to her stupid irrational OCD.

She has spent the whole day moaning, nagging, grumping and shouting at anything and everything. It has been an awful day and I just want to leave her. I just want to get away from her and all this. I want to be free of this complete nightmare, but I have no escape route. She keeps tight control on our money, so I have no way to do it.

She has been getting bigger and now she is so fat it is disgusting. She was once a size 10-12 but now she is an 18-20 or more with rolls of fat and massive thighs. Yuk!

Last night for example she was sulking in her room and ate a whole box of Pringles, a huge Toblerone bar and then a whole tub of guacamole with dipsticks!! So nowadays she not only is horrible and nasty, she looks horrible too.

June 1st 2014 18.00

Caroline hit Sacha on the head and grabbed a tennis ball off her and then threw it at her hurting her arm. I have no idea as to why but there can be no reason or justification.

Because of that I then shouted at her for hitting Sacha. Predictably she went mental at me. I totally thought she was going to hit me but instead she just grabbed my arms and dug her nails in.

She then spent a whole hour shouting and arguing with me before sulking back to her room and calling her mother.

She said she wanted a divorce. She said that because she was the woman and the mother that she would keep the house and everything else and therefore I'd end up with nothing and would have to pay for all that she had. Basically, this is a threat to blackmail me into just accepting her rubbish. She has used this threat many times but I am ready to call her bluff.

June 2nd 2014 08.00am

She got up and immediately started nagging me and ordering me around just like she does most mornings for whatever reason comes in to her head.

This time she was saying the house was a mess, probably her most common reason. What she means by a mess could actually be anything and quite generally is actually all about nothing. She is a perfectionist by proxy. In a way that she wants everything perfect but is too lazy to do the work so that means I have to do it.

Then a while later she went mental shouting at me because I burned Alice's sausages. She started shouting and calling me lots of names such as lizard eyes, small prick, stupid, lazy, and then because she wasn't getting the reaction she wanted she hit me again. This time it was a pretty decent slap to the face. Not the worst she has dealt me but still a right stinger and as much as anything taking this abuse and not giving anything back is tough on the ego and self-esteem.

After such an attack I generally feel so low and worthless. Sometimes I hurt myself just to numb the feeling or hit something just to let out some of the pent-up anger and frustration.

June 2nd 2014 09.30am

She gets up and started having a go at me. She carried on moaning and shouting at me for nearly two hours. It was all about the picnic we were going on and that I hadn't prepared any of the food for it the night before. Why hadn't I, what had I been doing all night? On and on over and over and then she threatened to call Tracey her friend and say we weren't going and it would be my fault.

June 5th 2014 08.00am

Caroline's period started late afternoon.

It seems like it is a bit like a release valve and so she was nice most of the day although probably because I spent 3 hours in the morning hoovering, tidying and moving furniture which always makes her happy as well as keeping me occupied and out of the way.

June 8th 2014 06.40am

When I got up I asked her a simple question. That question was "what should I give Alice for lunch", not a difficult question but she went mental at me. Shouting as to why didn't I do it the night before and what had I been doing all night bla bla bla. The same as she says every time. Am I not allowed to sleep at night?

She shouted at me for a full thirty minutes with me not even saying a word for the last twenty of them. I just stood there and let her abuse me and I just took it.

Then she turned on Sacha as she was not being quick enough in doing what she asked her to do.

June 10th 2014 20.00

She went mad at me at 8pm when I came up to the bedroom to ask her what she wanted to eat for tea. She was shouting at me because I had not made anything yet for us to eat.

Since she came home she had a shower, made herself a beef wrap, ate it and went to bed so it wasn't like she hadn't eaten anything.

Whilst she was in bed I put away the shopping (having to wipe off the germs off everything individually with antibacterial wipes) gave Alice her bath and played with her on the Wii. It wasn't like I did nothing.

June 12th 2014 22.00

When she came home from work she said nothing except that she had a go at me for putting a box on the toilet seat. Then demanded that she has her tea on the table when she comes in from work each day.

Later on, she came out the bedroom and started having a right go at me asking what had I been doing for the last two hours saying that I always faffed about at night and that she thought we might watch a film together.

However, she had just gone up to bed at about 7pm without saying a word so how was I supposed to know she wanted to spend such quality time with me.

I spent those two hours cleaning the kitchen, making kids lunches, sorting out the rubbish and recycling and printing out stuff for Sacha's school book project whilst she lay in bed upstairs and did nothing.

June 16th 2014 07.15am

Sacha would not get up out of bed and so Caroline started shouting at her then screamed at her.

Caroline went on and on at her and so Sacha then slapped Caroline on the arm. Caroline responded by hitting her and screaming at her, so I had to intervene. I got between them both and shouted at Caroline to stop. I sent Sacha back to her room and after a long stare and what looked like what was going to spark into her attacking me, Caroline turned and stormed off to her room.

June 17th 2014 19.00

Tonight, Caroline was shouting and arguing with Sacha about doing her homework.

Going on and on and being unfair. Pretty much a normal evening really.

June 18th 2014 22.00

Tonight, she has been absolutely f***ing mental. I came home from work to find the kids wandering outside and shouting, calling for food - this was at 6pm.

Caroline was upstairs in the shower and the kids were not allowed into the house and locked out just because they had been to the doctor's surgery and of course they were 'dirty' and infected.

I let them in and ran Alice's bath for her, so he could wash, and I then had to put her clothes in the wash straight away.

Caroline was in a foul mood and said as it was her birthday tomorrow and I had to bake her a cake tonight.

She kept going on about having a shit birthday all night even though her birthday had not even been.

I then had to go out twice to get things she wanted plus things for the cake. Then when I started to make the cake she said she wanted her tea and then went on and on and then stormed off upstairs in the end. Sacha and I prepared the cake put it in the oven then set out all the food and things for the raclette, so we could have a nice family meal for the eve of her birthday together.

Once it was all prepared and ready Sacha and I went upstairs and said to her that we were sorry and asked her to come down stairs. However, she refused saying it was a shit birthday again and again and told us to go and eat.

So we did, and then after a while we heard her shouting something upstairs but couldn't hear what she was saying. Then she came out her room and screamed at us to stop talking. So, we whispered but then she came out screaming at us to stop talking and that Sacha should go to bed even though this was only at 9.15pm.

Then I had about a 25 min tirade of abuse about it being a shit birthday and I should throw the cake in the bin and that I had made a mess and better clear it up and that I would have to take the kids to school in the morning and on and on and on and on so much that I was so close to just thumping her so I went and hid away from her in the utility room until she finally stormed back to her bedroom.

Wow, and her birthday is tomorrow so that should be fun!!??

June 19th 2014 07.00

Well after last night's shenanigans round 2 of Crazy Birthday Girl started as soon she got up and saw me. She was mental; shouting and blaming me for everything saying that I was shit and it was a shit birthday. Telling me I was useless. Shouting at me to do things then shouting at me for how I did them. She was just being so mean and nasty, saying the house was a mess even though I'd tidied it all up. She keeps saying things like "welcome to my world" bla bla bla. She seems to have totally forgotten how she ruined my birthday when she hit Alice etc...

Jun 20th 2014 09.30

Caroline was being quite nice this morning - obviously guilty about the last couple of days but she couldn't keep it up. Of course, she couldn't, she never can and never does. A small window of respite is the best we can hope for before the next event. It's a never-ending cycle and we are caught in the middle.

June 21st 2014 18.00

I came home to find her with a face like thunder and her first words to me as she glowered were "don't think you are going to football tonight there is loads to do and the place is a tip, my legs are hurting, and you need to do it all"

I cooked tea, tidied up and got Alice to bed, set up Sacha's homework and then went to my football. She is always trying to stop me going to football or doing anything that I enjoy. She is totally selfish and not interested in anyone's happiness but her own.

When I came back from football I tidied up, made the kids lunches and then emptied and refilled the dishwasher and cleaned up the kitchen. I had a bath and went to bed at about 11pm in the spare room, my room of course.

June 22nd 2014 06.30

Caroline got up, came downstairs to where I was and then started shouting at me.

Seemingly I had missed some things she wanted tidied up. These are things that I probably didn't even notice or didn't think were an issue. The sort of things that sit in her head and are never communicated until she sees them as a problem. So, I was subjected to a 40-minute tirade of shouting and abuse. The same sort of rubbish as she usually spits out of her stupid mouth about how useless I am and how she does everything. Telling me that I couldn't go kayaking tonight with Sacha as if she owns me and I have to do everything she says. Again, when I start to do something I like, in this instance it is kayaking with Sacha at a club, she has to try and stop me, us, from doing it. At first she encourages it. Go and do it, you like it, it will be fun. But when we are doing it and it is fun she tries to put a stop to it. For the last 16 years it has been the same. Anything I do or enjoy she puts a stop to it over time with her histrionics and manipulation. So much that I don't have any friends now.

I want out!

June 25th 2001 10.00

So, every Saturday I am up early to take Sacha and Alice swimming. I have been doing it since Sacha was 4. She won't do it because she is lazy for one and paranoid about getting a verruca from the pool.

Anyway, so she went mad at me and shouting when I came back from swimming saying that I hadn't tidied up last night.

For once it was actually true. I hadn't tidied up as I was tired, and I just watched TV. Meanwhile she spent all evening in the bedroom hiding away with her laptop and a pile of food. She does this every Friday, I think it must be because our nanny who comes to look after Alice has been here and she has infected the house downstairs. Crazy OCD mind that she has.

So, she went mad at me, shouting at me to do things. I filled Alice's bath as she has to have a bath straight after swimming even if he has had a shower there afterwards due to her OCD – in her mind the pool is dirty and infected, so he needs to be washed. So even though I had filled it up she told me to empty it. Meanwhile Alice took off her clothes in her bedroom and walked through to the bathroom. This sent her completely mental as he had 'dirty infected swimming pool feet' from being at the pool and so had contaminated the whole hallway and bathroom.

I picked Alice up, so she wasn't walking any longer on the floor, and was taking her back to her room but then I had to put her down because she was shouting at me. Then she came at me, screaming in my face and fists flying at me, hitting and punching me several times. Once she stopped hitting me she proceeded to hurl abuse and insults at me for another 20 minutes.

After this I just hit rock bottom and was in despair. It was all in front of Alice.

June 25th 2014 14.30 (later that same day)

She started going completely mental at me.

This was because we had some people come around and, in her mind, they had made the place dirty, so she said I had to mop the floor to make it all clean again.

So, I started to mop the floors but hadn't hoovered yet, so she shouted at me to hoover first. So, I stopped mopping the floor, got the hoover out and started hoovering up but then she started yelling at me to hoover only the carpets and not the floor tiles for some reason only known to her.

When I said no she attacked me and started hitting me, so I pushed her away from me. She was screaming and flailing her arms at me and swearing. Once she sopped hitting me she carried on hurling abuse at me and shouting at me for half an hour.

I put my headphones on and put music on to drown her noise out and ignore her. She didn't like this one bit because I was not reacting to her shouting and moaning. So, then she then came right up to my face and started screaming at me again and then she grabbed the headphone cable and ripped them out of my ears really hurting me as they were the sports sort that wrap around your ears and the bud goes inside. Then she went on and on at me for ages and ages. I tried my best to ignore her again. She was saying the usual rubbish and saying I never did anything with the kids or any housework and I was shit!

June 26th 2014 20.00

She started going mental at me as I put down some baby wipes that were lying around in the bathroom with the baby changing kit.

Seemingly this was the wrong place and I deserved half an hour tirade of abuse and insults – lucky me.

July (again)

July 2nd 2014 15.00

I just endured half an hour of ranting and abuse from her all because when I went to the Co-op I bought Alice some biscuits. Not a crime in itself but seemly the fact that they contained palm oil really is a crime. She is moaning and complaining about everything I do or have done since birth.

This is just complete mental torture going on and on at me like this very day it seems for absolutely nothing. I don't know how long I can take this for. It's like she is trying to break me and turn me into a jelly or something. I have no idea how to make her stop as I think I have tried every imaginable approach. Shouting back doesn't work, walking away doesn't work, staying silent and ignoring her doesn't work, hiding myself in a room and keeping the door closed doesn't work, nothing works it just keeps on coming at me relentlessly.

I am trapped in an abusive relationship. I am trapped in an abusive marriage. I am being abused mentally, emotionally, physically and verbally.

If I was a woman there would be all sorts of help and support out there for me. Somewhere to go. Someone to talk to, someone that could and would help me. But for me there is nothing and nobody anywhere, nowhere to turn. As a man there seems to be no help, no support, no outlet.

Some days she is great and lovely. In fact, she was nice earlier today, but she turns like a snake in the grass and goes mental in the blink of an eye. There is something wrong with her as this is definitely not normal

I feel like I am stuck back at school being bullied and beasted with nowhere to escape and nowhere to hide.

It is times like this is when I really hate her. I wouldn't ever let anyone else speak to me the way she does so why should I just accept it? I would not accept it at work, in the street or anywhere else. This is so unfair and undeserved as I work so bloody hard at work and at home for this family.

If I leave I lose everything, it is so unfair!! I don't have much choice, leaving is the only way but I can't leave the kids and she will never let me take them. Why does the man always lose everything?

July 3rd 2014 10.00am

She has just gone to work and thank god for that. It's Sunday and we just love our Sundays without her. It is something all 3 of us look forward to.

We can't go to church now because of all the things she has made me do so far this morning. We are not dressed or ready and all the stuff she has told me to do means I'll spend all day doing housework - if I don't do it I'll get a tirade of abuse later. So far this morning it has been moan, moan, nag, nag, and I just can't take another night of the same.

We go to church every Sunday. Or at least we used to. She now doesn't want to go when she is off and so that means we can't go either because we have to do what she wants. Now we just go every second Sunday when she works or when I am doing my turn at Sunday school. Now it seems like she is going to start making such a fuss about Sundays too so that I can't even go at all. Same as she does with anything else I do like the football, golf and kayaking and every other thing I try to do.

Now she had gone we can have a nice day together until she comes back, and she may be nice for a while but watch this space. Funny – we all hate Saturdays but love alternate Sundays!

Sunday 3rd July 2014 11.00am

I have just been thinking about all the things that I used to do or wanted to do that she has stopped me doing:

Golf: I used to play but now I'm not allowed to. Last year I played a few games secretly whilst away on business and that was it.

Snowboarding: I haven't been away for years and now she won't even let me go to the snow place at Castleford on my birthday which is the only time I have been able to go for the last few years. Earlier in the year I went a couple of times in London when I was away and staying overnight there with work. This was again done secretly as if I told her she would have gone mental at me for doing something for me or spending the money on something.

Mountain biking: I used to go out riding around the area, but she moans at me anytime I try to go. I used to go with my brother but that's not allowed either.

Football: I used to play a lot, but she stopped me doing it. I am now not allowed to go to training or consider a match or joining a club. I now play with some dads on a Tuesday night in the town park but each time she tells me I can't go, that I must do x or y at home instead but recently I have been going anyway. Ignoring her and then normally to find her in bed in a huff and the house a mess expecting me to tidy it all up when I get back.

Kayaking - recently started doing this again with Sacha on a Wednesday evening in Catterick but again it is always a battle about going and she says I can't go as a threat or punishment every second day to me or Sacha. Also, every time I want to go out in the evening for a paddle in our own kayak she moans and says no and gives me jobs to do.

Cricket: I used to play for the church team a few times a year on a Sunday afternoon but she made it so unbearable when I did play the few times these last years, telling me I can't go when previously saying I could, ringing me up when playing telling me to come home as I'd been out too long and stupid stuff like that and so this last year I have not played at all as she would not let me.

Running: I used to get up extra early for a run, but I am not allowed as it disturbs her she said to go in the evening and when I do she says no or nags.

Church: I try to go most Sundays, but she tells me not to and gives me things to do - she says I only go to get rid of the kids and have an hour doing nothing and being lazy.

Going out for a drink with friends: As for that then I have only been out once in the last few years for a quick pint with Mark as when I do, again she makes such a fuss and I have to do so much to make up for it all

I have to ask for permission to do anything and then it is almost always denied. This makes me feel like a grounded and controlled teenager and totally frustrates me.

I totally understand the need to do less stuff for me and do more stuff for the family but to be not allowed to do anything at all ever is just not fair or right. It's what I already do as I do so much for and with the family anyway.

On her two days off when the kids are at school she can do whatever she likes and in actual fact she does. I don't interfere with that and never complain. I didn't even try she'd just go mad at me anyway.

Tomorrow night she has agreed for me to stay overnight away in London, so I can take my team out for a thank you meal - I wonder how she will kick off with me being away and going out at night - watch this space.

Sunday 3rd July 18.00 (later same night)

As I expected she was nice for half an hour then started moaning at me and having a go at me for what I'd made for tea then a load of things I haven't done yet and telling me I couldn't stay overnight in London or be home late.

Tues 5th July 2014 5pm

The minute I walked in the door from work she started having a
go at me. It started because I had left my shoes on a mat by the
back door. Then she started shouting at me to make tea, but
she didn't tell me or give me any clue as to what I was meant to
be cooking, what she had bought or what she had in mind for
me to cook. Then she started going mad at me about hand
washing and touching things in the kitchen even though I had
worn gloves to sort the chicken out for tea. I had to wear gloves
and wash my hands due to the potential for cross
contamination and possible salmonella spreading. As
mentioned before in her sick mind all chicken is covered in
germs and salmonella and so unless all these rules are followed
we would die a horrendous death. The fact that I had worn
gloves and washed my hands still didn't seem enough for her as
I obviously hadn't done it to her exact satisfaction.

She then said I didn't have a clue about all the things that
needed done at home after collecting kids from school. When I
pointed out that I have done it already for so many times on
every Friday she said what I did was shit and the place was
never organised and always a mess. She said the kids had been

143

driving her mental with fighting and arguing and asking for things since they got in which is of course my fault because I wasn't there to do it all and she was having to do something herself.

Then she started having a go at me and complaining about me leaving her to look after the kids whilst I was away from home for work and going out for meals with people from work. I knew it wouldn't take long for that subject to come up as it was lying under the surface for days. In fact, it only took 20 minutes from me walking in the door to her yelling about it.

Sacha took Alice away to play so that they were away from her to protect and distract her. I asked Sacha how it had been the last few days since I was away, and Sacha said she had been crazy. Shouting about everything at both of them but luckily, she didn't hit her. Then Caroline ordered me to tidy Alice's room up. Why I have no idea, she just wanted to continue the argument and make a scene ordering me around. When I said no she said I couldn't have any of the tea or food that she had prepared nor was I allowed to eat any of the food in the fridge as I had not left her with any after the weekend when I left and I'd used up all the food making her a sh*t couscous meal the other night. A complete nutter as usual but then her friend, her only friend, called her and when she answered and talked to her she was all sweetness and light. Acting like the complete schizophrenic Jackal and Hyde person that she is.

Tues 5th July 2014 6pm

She started yelling and screaming at Alice because she made a mess in the hallway. She then spent the whole next hour just shouting at us all about everything and being unreasonable.

Tues 5th July2014 21.05

I came back from football at 5 minutes past 9 in the evening and she went totally mad at me. She started shouting at me and asking why was I so late (normally I'm in at about 9pm). Asking when did football finish and that the fact I went to get some milk from the shop on the way back was no excuse for being so late.

She was yelling at me saying that I was selfish and did nothing in the house at all and that she did everything which was the only reason that made it possible for me to do sports. She said that from now on I'm not allowed to play football anymore. When responded by saying I can do whatever I like, and she can't order me about, she went really crazy at me. Calling me names, saying that she wasn't a pushover like my mum, that she was going to stop doing things around the house completely and that she would make me take the kids to school two times a week rather than the agreed once a week – bearing in mind I work over an hour away.

She continued yelling at me about everything and anything that came into her head as she usually does. About me not washing my hands properly. About me driving the new BMW, saying I took it just to show off at work about having a nice car. Every time I walked away, tried to move away from her or went to another room to get away from her, she followed me shouting and yelling at me.

Sacha then came down from bed and asked her to be quiet as she was disturbing her from sleeping. I told Caroline that she was totally out of order and needed to get help as she was out completely of control and needed to stop this abuse. But of course, as usual, she denied it all and just continued following me and yelling at me. I put my hands over my ears to drown out her noise, but she was yelling and screaming right in my face calling me a loony and saying it was me who needed to see a psychiatrist. She was dancing in front of me and at me, goading me and yelling in my face. I just looked at her and laughed at her and said you look ridiculous like a total crazy clown. She did not like that one bit, but it did the trick and she stormed off to her bedroom, slamming the door.

Wow, I really thought she was going to hit me again that time, but she is so clever and manipulative. I wanted her to hit me this time because I had made my mind up that if she did I was going to phone the police and report her although I don't know if I really would have when it came to it, but I so wanted to.

This is getting totally out of hand. Her behaviour is awful and getting increasingly worse as time goes on. I am walking on eggshells all the time!

Tonight, when I was out at football for a whole 80 minutes, I was out I had fun and forgot about everything that was going on at home. I enjoyed myself and it was great but then I walked into that! There is no way I am giving up my football no matter what she says.

Tues 5th July 2014 22.45

I spent hours trawling the net looking for help, support and some kind of ideas as to what might be going on. I was trying to make sense of it all and in the end, I think I found what is wrong with her. I think she has potentially NPD (Narcissistic Personality Disorder) or perhaps BPD (Borderline Personality Disorder) - the symptoms and signs are all there. She seems to display all the traits they describe and follows the exact patterns and format although its not easy to distinguish for me if she is Borderline or Narcissistic.

I posted my first post on a website called Soul2Soul and told my story for the first time which has really helped. I may have found a start to be able to deal with this.

Wednesday 6th July 2014 7.10am

She got up this morning all sweetness and light and was reading a book with Alice so nicely but then suddenly she stopped and started having a go at me right where she left off the previous night like a stuck record. She was saying that I was selfish and that I do nothing around the house. That I had to sort out all the food and everything for Alice's birthday party. That I was giving her cheese for lunch when there is nothing else in the house for her to eat but that is my fault as I didn't do any shopping whilst at work or away for work. She shouted at me for having breakfast and not doing various housework tasks that she wanted me to do. She went on and on for ages, meanwhile being nice to the kids but with a real visible effort only.

She stopped for a few minutes and was in her bedroom but then she started up again at me going on and on saying the same things as before trying to wind me up and make me angry. She was doing all this in front if the kids, so I would argue in front of them, but I did my best to ignore it. Again, it was mental and like torture.

Wednesday 6th July 2014 23.00

Tonight, she has been more or less ok, almost human and acting as if nothing ever happened the last few days but that was because the Nanny was here, and we were at the secondary school.

However, later on that night she just came out of her room asking what the hell I was doing downstairs and why hadn't I done everything that needed doing so she told me she was going to sleep, and I could get lost.

Not as per her normal rage, a lot calmer than usual but a turn of personality again none the less.

Thursday 7th July 2014 19.30

Sacha had not eaten her lunch so was sent to her bedroom as a punishment. After tea Sacha refused to go to her bedroom so Caroline shouted at her to go. When she didn't go Caroline screamed in her face at her to go upstairs. When Sacha still refused to go Caroline slapped her on the bottom then tried to drag her off her seat and towards the stairs pulling her violently as she did so. I stepped in before it escalated as it was heading that way and I sent, or rather asked Sacha to go to her room to resolve the situation.

Thursday 7th July 2014 20.45

She came upstairs and found me sitting down in my bedroom, the back bedroom, and started yelling at me about what was I doing sitting and doing nothing and why was I sitting down when so many things need to be done. I had been sat for a maximum of 10 minutes whilst she had been sat down on her computer for an hour at least downstairs. She shouted at me to get some shopping from the Co-op that closes at 9pm which meant I only had 15 minutes. When I asked what she wanted me to buy there she started yelling at me again saying that I didn't know because I was leaving it all to her. So, she gave me a list and was still shouting at me after I went out the door, as I could hear her as I went towards the car.

It is Alice's party on Saturday and tomorrow night we have to prepare everything so watch this space - she will kick off again I am certain of it and so it just depends on how badly this time. She always goes crazy at these things.

Saturday 9th July 2001 11.30am

Last night and this morning has been pretty much ok despite all the preparations for Alice's party food preparation, making cakes, sandwiches, biscuits, fruit and vegetables all sorted with little comment. She has been on her best behaviour up until we set off to the sports centre - I knew it wouldn't last.

We were in the car about 2 minutes down the road when she asked if I had brought the iPod with us, which I hadn't. She then asked if I had brought the Sellotape, but I hadn't.

She then went mad at me and told me to turn the car round and go back for them shouting at me saying I was an idiot and useless and that all I had to do was bring some Sellotape and I couldn't even do. She said she did all the work for the party and the only things I did were all because she laid them on a plate for me to do.

We got back to the house and I went in as quick as I could to get the iPod speakers and the Sellotape but after about 1 minute she was in at the door yelling at me to hurry up and why was I taking so long and that I was too f**king slow and f**king useless. She was shouting this all very loudly at me outside our house for all the neighbours to hear.

When we got back in the car she laid on another tirade of abuse about how shit I was and how I didn't do anything, and she did it all. She said if I were a single parent the kids would never have a party as I'd never be able to organise it. She said it was because my parents were useless that I never had parties as a kid and just went on and on saying the same things and being so offensive and abusive.

I just made some noises like I was paying attention and smiled to myself and it was great as I knew exactly what she was doing, and I didn't bite at all which really spooked her - I was so proud of my non-reaction. Having discovered what her issue was, the NPD/BPD and read some ways of trying to deal with it I felt far more empowered as I smiled to myself and let her get on with her craziness. They say knowledge is power and it seemed that was so true at that moment.

For about 19 minutes as we drove to the venue she just banged on and on about the same old rubbish and saying I was driving too slowly, then too fast and it made no matter what ever I said or did it was all wrong. But it's her who is wrong, completely wrong in the head.

Saturday 9th July 2001 23.30

Tonight has been ok, I didn't take any of the bait on her usual jibes and insults. I just carried on doing what I was doing and ignored her which she hated.

She went up for a shower at about 7.30pm and then went straight to bed with her iPad to surf her 'Kidsmums' website drivel whilst I (the lazy good for nothing useless husband) cleared up the kitchen, bathed Alice, played with Alice, gave her her supper and put her to bed which is pretty much what I do every night. Not bad for a lazy good for nothing useless husband.

I then went out for a cycle ride - 45 mins and 10 miles which was a great release. When I came back I didn't get shouted at for once as she was still in bed surfing and watching tv and I went nowhere near her. I had a bath then did the ironing (again, as I do every week) and watched a film on TV. Compared to last week this was bliss, at least she was nowhere near me or saying anything to me.

These bits of respite can easily make you think that it is all ok and her outbursts and violence is all due to things I've done but it isn't at all like that. It is her fault and totally unpredictable, unacceptable and a ticking bomb waiting to go off anytime

I think she is trying hard as she knows she really upset me last weekend and since then I have continued to sleep in the spare room but it's not working on me. I am as stubborn as they come when I want to be.

Sunday 10th July 2014 8.30am

She just came downstairs and started going on at me about a load of weeds in the garden and told me to sort them out as the garden is my responsibility. I asked her when does she expect me to do that? She said I should have done it one evening and as an example I could have done it last night instead of going for a cycle. She says she does everything in the house and I should do the garden as I only do a few little things in the house. Like that's so, so true.

She told me to do it this afternoon and when I said I wanted to do something with the kids instead she said all I wanted to do was go for a walk to the park like I always do and it's all for myself and not for them, but I just take them because I was selfish.

She then said I should do it now and not go to church again - I think she is trying to keep me away from people and again looking for any excuse to stop me going to church. So now I will go out in the garden and do it but just to get away from her. So, I get dressed and ready to go out to garden as she wanted me to do but then she says, "what are you doing?". I say I'm going to do the grading like you told me to. She then replies, "I didn't say do it now, I said you could do it now. But now I want you to come and read a book with Alice as she won't do it with me.".

Alice was lying on the floor saying "I don't want to read a book with you I want to do it with Daddy", and she was yelling at her, but she was lying there saying bla bla bla to her which she really hates.

Monday 11th July 2014 07.25am

She shouted at Alice and called her stupid because she didn't write her name properly. A totally unacceptable way to talk to a young child. It is definitely going to give her confidence issues, no wonder she stammers when she talks.

Mon 11th July 2014 18.00

Came home to my tea all ready for me when I came in - that's a first!! Just makes me wonder what she is playing at, what is she after?

Tues 12th July 2014 11.00

I contacted a solicitor who called me back and I have booked an appointment for next Thursday to understand my options. All the research I have done tells me I need to get out of this marriage.

Tues 12th July 2014 14.30

I rang the helpline called Mankind which is supposed to be for men in abusive situations and told my story to them. I talked with a wonderful lady who was very understanding and very helpful giving me great advice.

Tues 12th July 2014 21.00

Tonight, I went out and played football as normal despite being told I was not allowed to anymore last week.

She was ok when I went out but really grumpy when I came back. She started giving me jobs to do and criticising how I was doing things and then going on about how I was washing my hands and touching bins in her usual OCD way.

Weds 13th July 2014 18.10

Caroline started shouting at Sacha to shut up because she was crying because Caroline said we were not allowed to go kayaking tonight because Alice has her school play and I have to pick her up at 8.20 even though she was at home and could easily do it. She gave no reason as to why she couldn't do it. So, she was yelling at Sacha to get out of the kitchen, which she refused and so Caroline kicked her in the leg. When I confronted her with this she said she only kicked her softly and it was because she refused to get out. Then she started having a go at me, so I walked away. A kick is a kick and its abuse.

Weds 13th July 2014 19.00

When I came back from taking Alice to her school play (I took Sacha with me too as I didn't want to leave her with Caroline alone in the house) Caroline was in her bedroom and didn't come out when we came back which was lucky.

Wednesday 13th July 2014 20.55

When I came back from picking Alice up, Caroline came out her room. She told Sacha to go and tidy the playroom and when Sacha refused to do it she shouted in her face calling her a stupid cow and a cheeky bitch.

When Sacha came back upstairs Caroline stormed out of her bedroom and screamed at Sacha in her face saying what do you think you're doing you stupid little cow.

Wednesday 13th July 2014 21.15-22.15

I have just spent the last hour talking with and consoling my daughter about what has been happening to her and the affect all this abuse is having. This really cut me up – Sacha is in a bad state and this has affected her even more than I had imagined and even more than me probably because she is so young and it's her mother, not some stranger.

Sacha worries the whole time and reacts badly to simple things at school which alienates her and now she is being bullied at school too. This is all because of Caroline.

I need to take action and get this sorted out ASAP as this is killing our souls and turning us into scared and anxious people. An 11-year-old girl should be loved and embraced as a child not subjected to this hell by her own mother.

I feel like such a terrible father for not doing anything about this before and letting it happen to my children who I hold dearest in the whole world. It will be painful to take their mother away but if I don't then who knows the damage and pain that will be caused?

I can't take any more of this from her, so how can they? I will not leave them in her reign of terror, I must not, and I cannot. Tonight, I would have called the police, but I don't have all my ducks in a row, but I will do so very soon indeed.

Today I was going to contact the police, but it dawned on me that doing so will destroy her career as well as everything else as she won't be able to do her job if this comes out. But now I don't give a f**k anymore about her as she is destroying my little girl which is deplorable, and she deserves everything that will be coming to her, but I will do it by the book with my business head on and not just pure emotion.

The most cutting thing that Sacha said to me tonight whilst in tears was - "I'm turning into her!"

An NPD/BPD nurtures the next generation of NPD/BPD - I must stop it before it is too late.

PART 3 – EPLILOGUE

So, there you have it. You have now read the diary, a catalogue of actual incidents and feelings.

Was this normal?

What do you think?

What would you do?

I suppose you can now see why I started the diary? Perhaps you'd like to know what happened next, what came after the diary? Please read on because the story is by no means over. Not by a long way yet.

Why Did I stop the Diary then?

So, why didn't I just carry on with the diary? Why did I stop
then? I stopped the diary at that point because firstly my eyes
were fully opened to the fact that something needed to be
done, I needed to take action. I had written and recorded
enough, and we could not carry on like that any longer. Above
all, I needed to protect the children and myself. The discussion
that night on the 13th of July with Sacha broke my heart but
steeled my resolve. I had to do something, this had to stop.

I had already started to reach out to some men's support
agencies and discovered about her true nature, about why she
acts the way she does and that she may have some kind of
disorder like Borderline Personality Disorder or Narcissistic
Personality Disorder. The information and advice I had was
leading me to look at taking legal action as there was little
alternative. I was unsure of what to do, where to start and
where to go.

Then, the next time I was away from home, which was the
following Monday night, I synchronised my phone with my
laptop and therefore had all the notes that I had made on my

phone in my diary on the laptop. I then cut and pasted each and every single entry from the diary into a single word document. In doing so I was reading and reliving the previous year. I counted 34 times she had been violent towards me and 18 towards one of the children. If nothing else had woken me up before now, then this did. I was so upset, I knew I had to do something.

I contacted the local police helpline for domestic violence which was independently run and made an appointment to see them. I also called me local police station and booked an appointment to see someone there. The advice I'd been given from the forum was to log the background, history and incidents with the police, just in case they were called to our home by her or me at a later stage. Then they would not be coming to the house blind, they would know the history and therefore not just accept what she might say at the time. I also booked in to see my GP to tell him what was happening – another recommendation from the forum.

The first of these appointments was with the GP and he was totally useless. I went there and told him I was being abused, yet all he was interested in was the children and reporting the situation to Social Services. That wasn't what I needed at that time as I didn't need to have social services involved, I intended to handle it myself. I managed to persuade him to hold off any reporting as I was handling it and he agreed for the time being.

Then I went to the local police and the officer I saw was very good and understanding. He logged the situation and I gave them a stripped-down fact only copy of my log with all the incidents. I removed the emotions and story around each incident. I later sent an electronic copy to them too for their records.

Then I went to the support centre in Harrogate and they were very helpful and supportive. They normally only get women but have had a few men and so they were not unused to my situation. Their advice was that I really had to get out of the marriage and take the children. Their opinion is that an abuser is always an abuser and will not change. They recommended a solicitor who was based next door rather than the one I'd already spoken to. So, I went to the solicitors and made an appointment. When I saw them, they recommended a course of action that involved taking out several court orders to stop her abuse, remove her from the home and obtain custody of the children. All very drastic action and I went to consider how to do all this and when. The orders were an Anti-molestation order to stop her violence. A Residency order for the children to live with me and an Occupancy order effectively removing her from the home.

What happened next?

When I had been speaking with Sacha that night, I had said to her that it might help her if she talked to one of her friends at school about her mum hitting her. This is something that she actually went and did. The friend she chose to talk to, had a mother who was a school teacher in another school. The child told the mother what was going on and then the mother, because she was concerned, contacted Sacha's school.

One thing led to another and the next day, while I was at work, I had a distraught call from Caroline telling me that she had been called into the school from the head teacher and she had been summoned to go and see her. When she got there, she discovered that there had been a report from the friend's mother about her hitting Sacha and that Sacha had been interviewed and confirmed it was true.

When I got home, Caroline was in pieces and pleaded with me to go to the school and tell them it wasn't true, and it was all blown out of proportion. That I had to tell them it was just normal chastisement, and that Sacha was making a fuss about nothing.

So, I went to the school and met with the head teacher, but I didn't tell them the story Caroline wanted me to say. I told them the truth, that it had been going on and that I had been in touch with the police, support agencies and that I was in the process of dealing with the problem. The head teacher accepted this and left me to deal with the problem for now, as long as I did deal with it.

I went back home and then later with the kids out of the way, I gave Caroline hell. I actually had some factual evidence and information that backed my situation that I was able to speak to her about. I said that it was enough, she was out of order and that she had to leave. I told her it was not normal, she was abusive and that it was now all over. She pleaded and pleaded with me. She promised never to hit the children again and never to hit me again. Eventually, she wore me down, I gave in and with all her promises I gave her a final chance. I told her that if anything happens again that I'd go to the police and throw her out. She talked with Sacha and apologised and promised her she would never do it again.

She seemed genuine and very remorseful and I fell for it all. I backed down and stopped the legal action I was planning. For a while things settled down and were as calm and normal as I'd ever known them to be. She was on her best behaviour and we had about a month of normal family life and it was blissful.

Then at the end of August we went on holiday to Spain to stay at an apartment where we had been the previous year. Most of the holiday was good and Caroline was on pretty good behaviour, but two things happened that were the final straw for me. The first was in the swimming pool. She was playing around with Sacha in a crowded pool and Sacha flicked some water in her face. Caroline was wearing her glasses and they got wet. She went mental and grabbed Sacha by the arm, twisted it and pushed her head under water holding her there. The look of pure venom on her face was hideous. I was only a few metres away watching them and swam across as quickly as I could, grabbed Sacha out from under the water and shoved Caroline out of the way.

Sacha was so traumatised by this it took me ages to calm her and console her. Whereas Caroline was laughing and pretending it was all a joke, that it was just a piece of fun. However, I had seen the look on her face. I knew it was no joke. She lost her temper yet again and lost control. She went over the top and was once again out of order.

Then on the last day, when we were packing to head back home I put away a toy mace in one of the suitcases, but I didn't wipe it with antibacterial wipes nor put it in a bag before putting in in the suitcase. She saw that I had done this and went crazy at me shouting and calling me names just like before. And when I responded with "yes, so whatever" she punched me in the stomach with full force which really hurt me. For me that was the final straw, she promised never to hit me again and she had. She promised never to hurt the kids but she nearly drowned Sacha. I went next door and told our friends who were staying there what she had done and showed them the big red mark on my stomach. They were appalled. We then journeyed home with hardly a word spoken between us, but I had made my mind up that action needed to be taken.

When I was back at work on the Monday I started to put the plans I had back in July into action. I contacted my solicitor and made an appointment. My support network all backed me up with what to do. I met with my solicitor and put the process and paperwork in place to take her to court and obtain the 3 court orders. Anti-molestation orders, a Residency order and Occupancy orders for her to be removed from the home and me to have custody of the children. On the Friday the 5th of September I went to court to obtain the orders. I never thought for one moment the significance of the date – it was the day we first met. At that time I was just focussed on what needed to be done and paid no attention to the dates.

The Legal System.

I agonised through that whole week about if I was doing the right thing or not. I prayed and sought a sign from God and believed it was the only way forward. I nearly backed out a few times, but I knew I had to go through with it. Instead of going to work on that Friday I went to the local Family Courts in Harrogate.

I went before the judge with my barrister. The judge said he was not convinced enough to give the temporary orders without any input or discussion with Caroline. He gave a temporary anti-molestation order to stop her hitting me or the kids but deferred both other orders to a full court hearing on the following Tuesday.

What he said to me was that he was not convinced as it was such a big and unusual thing for me to be asking for as I was a man. He said he knew that it was going to be a very difficult few days for me but that I had to return to the family home and stay there until we both attended court on Tuesday. Meanwhile she would be served the temporary anti-molestation order and a court summons to appear at court on Tuesday later that evening when she was back from work.

So, I trusted in the law to protect me and the children from this crazy woman and they let me down. I had to go home and wait for her to come home and be served the papers. She was going to go completely crazy and I was so scared. I had done the hardest thing I had ever had to do, something that despite all she had done to us was still breaking my heart. However, I was not given the backing I needed from the court. I was left hung out to dry.

I never felt so low, so alone and abandoned ever in my life. I had nowhere to go and no one to turn to. I had done this all on my own so far and had no real support. I never even told my parents what I was planning or had done.

The funfair was in town that day, so I took the kids to it and waited for her to come home and get served the papers. When we went out the guy was waiting with the papers to serve to her. I was so anxious. I wandered around the fair with the kids in a trance like state, so sacred of what she was going to do.

Then at almost 7pm she called me. She wasn't screaming but saying "Jim, Jim, Jim what have you done, what have you done, what is all this? Why, why, why?" Over and over again. She was hysterical but not aggressive. She asked me to come home, so we could talk and with so much reluctance and a heavy heart I headed home with the children to face her.

When I got there she just said the same things again and again. Saying "Jim, Jim, Jim what have you done, what have you done, what is all this? Why, why, why?" She poured on the guilt and played the innocent victim. She did not shout or get angry or violent as I had expected which was very surprising. Then she called her mother and then her brother called, and it just carried on and on like that all night. She was keeping me up all night talking and pleading me to stop it all and retract everything. Trying to wear me down again and saying that she would lose her job and livelihood, that I was destroying her life. I went to try and escape from her in my bedroom, but she just would not let me be. She would not let me sleep and kept on all night.

The next day her mother, brother and his wife turned up all to convince me that I should drop it all and retract the statements and we could solve it within the family.

Interestingly, during the various discussions her brother pulled me to the side and told me she knew exactly what Caroline was like and said he was pleased that someone had finally stood up to her and held her accountable for her actions and behaviour but that this way was not how we did it in the family. They went on and on at me for two days and two nights until they finally wore me down and I agreed to retract it all. Caroline promised never to do anything like that again and we could move on. I was totally broken by this point and could see no alternative. She was being extra nice and making so many promises and pleading that we would make it all work.

On Monday I instructed my solicitor to withdraw and retract it all and she said she would inform the court but that we would still both have to go to the court on the Tuesday for the hearing in any case.

On Tuesday we went to court together and sat together. I confirmed that I wanted to withdraw it all and I said that I had

179

got things out of proportion. It wasn't a small room like I was in on the Friday, this was the full proper crown court like affair with barristers and lots of people in the public gallery. It was pretty scary, and Caroline absolutely hated the whole thing. It gave her a real shock and if anything was going to make her stop her abuse then this was going to be it.

The judge said he was not ready to dismiss the case without a report on the safety of the children from The Children and Family Court Advisory and Support Service (Cafcass) and adjourned the hearing until the report was compiled. So, we left with this whole thing still hanging over us and the last thing that Caroline would have wanted – social services coming in and asking questions.

A week or so later, we were both interviewed by Cafcass, as were the school and some others about the situation. I played it all down as instructed, and Caroline was sweetness and light. The report said there was no specific evidence of real danger to the children. We then went back to court and this time we were in the Judge's chambers where a lady judge finally dismissed the case and told us to get some counselling next time and not to go to court.

This chapter was over, and we could now get back to our normal lives. She won, I was broken.

After all this we settled back to normal life and for a while Caroline was on her best behaviour and it looked like things would be ok. Then things did properly return to normal. The normal abuse and rules and shouting started after some time, and her behaviour actually got worse. Her OCD was increasing, and the violence came back. She was no longer violent towards the children, but she was from time to time violent towards me.

18 months later.

So, let's wind on a while and see how things were after my completely failed attempt at stopping the abuse and escaping from the nightmare using the legal system.

Quite simply I was back where I started. The abuse and control were still there, her OCD was as bad as ever and now she had another rod with which to beat me and control me. Now I had been so bad and awful to her by taking her to court that I needed to make up for it. I needed to grovel and do everything. I needed to do more round the house and pander to everything she wanted.

It was marginally better for the children, so I had accomplished something but for me, she laid on the guilt and manipulation thick day in day out. My life was not my own. I was a shell of my former self. I had tried and failed, and I felt worthless with nowhere to turn. I wanted to leave her, but I had nowhere to go. No one to talk to or to turn to. I even bowed out of my support forum because all they told me to do was to leave her. I knew it was the only way, but I was too weak.

To cap it all; in December 2015 I lost my job. I had then tried to deal with my boss who was also a bully. It was a choice of she went, or I went, and in the end I went although I did get paid off well. Caroline took this as another weapon to beat me up with. Even though she hated the job I had and the fact I was an hour's drive away at each end of the day and the fact my boss was always making me work late and go to London she still used the situation to ridicule me and bully me and tell me I was a piece of rubbish.

I used the money from the payoff to keep us going whilst I re-started my consultancy business. It took only a few weeks for me to get some work. As soon as my contacts knew I was available, the work came. I was ok. I was able to earn enough to keep things going and work less – only 3 to 4 days a week. I got a good long-term contract and so I was able to work from home a lot and take the pressure off by looking after the kids and the home. However, as predicted nothing I did was ever good enough for her. The more I did the more she demanded and expected and the more opportunity she had to have a go at me, shout at me and chastise me like a naughty child.

Whilst looking for contracts I had the potential for a great job in Bahrain. I flew out there for an interview and was offered an initial 3-month contract with expenses paid. It was an amazing opportunity.

However, Caroline refused. She would not move the family out there and would not let me take the job and work away on my own. So, I was unable to take the job. It was always her way or no way. This was another example of the control she wielded over my life.

The other thing that she used to control me was sex. Basically, she withheld sex almost all the time. It started after Alice was born but it carried on for years. Basically, we never had sex during a period of about 4 years in total. Our marriage was completely sexless. She would use the lure or promise of sex but then always withdraw it as a punishment. Or she just couldn't be bothered. At the same time her laziness coupled with overeating made her balloon, so she wasn't attractive any longer, so I gave up and stopped even trying to have sex.

Emotionally this was very damaging. The rejection was terrible, and it made my feeling of worthlessness even greater. Through all these years it was only my work and time with the kids that kept me going and made it bearable. I loved my kids and doing things with them. When I was at work, I had an escape and an outlet to be away from her. It made it bearable.

One night during an argument I called her frigid and said she was fat and ugly. I said look in the mirror and see what you have done to yourself. This was not something I'm proud of but with her goading there were always times when I'd break and retaliate. It was impossible not to and I always tried not to because that meant when I did she was able to play the victim card and use it against me again.

Then she said, "go and get your sex elsewhere, go and find yourself someone for that because you are not getting it from me ever". A rather shocking a thing for your wife to say but you know what, I was in such a place at the time that I thought, "what the hell, I'll go and do just that".

I saw it as a means to an escape from her because when I did find it elsewhere then with her monitoring of me she would find out and then the marriage would be over, and freedom would ensue. A way to escape the living nightmare.

At this point we had been married 17 years and I had been completely faithful during that whole time. I believed in the sanctity of marriage, especially as we had a full white wedding in a church. I believed that you marry for life and even though I could have had an affair before, as opportunities had presented themselves to me over the years, I never took them because that wasn't me. But this time I actually went looking. I knew what I was looking for and it didn't take me long to find it.

The internet and the affair

This part of the journey is not a pretty story in any way on my part and is something I am not proud of, even though at the time it was exactly what I needed and wanted. It is a period that I should shut away and forget about but it's also important to understand what I did and why. So yes, after her rant at me I decided I was going to go looking for sex.

I wasn't going to go and pay for it, I wasn't going to go to a prostitute or anything like that. I went online and joined a couple of raunchy websites for married people looking for extra marital encounters. These were paid for sites that were above board but very open about what they were about. They were for people who were married who wanted some fun on the side. Sometimes it was just chatting, talking, sharing photos and potentially hook ups.

I enjoyed the chase. The excitement of talking with some other women who were interested in me after so much rejection was a real boost. Having been told I was useless, ugly and that no other woman would ever be interested in me, it gave me confidence. I chatted with some, flirted, shared naked pics and did some sex talk. I was looking for someone in a similar situation to me who just was bored and wanted some no strings fun and sex. This was not who I was, but it was what I needed then at that time. It gave me some spark in my otherwise dead life. It made me realise that I was not like the things she said I was.

So, whilst chatting with a woman called Amy, we hit it off. We got on well and we chatted a lot. We swapped numbers and then moved to talking on the phone. We swapped pics and had some video calls. Then after about ten days we met up for a drink. She lived a few hours away from me, so we met somewhere in the middle. That was actually a proper date. We had a few drinks, we ate some food, we talked, we fancied each other, and we kissed. She was a couple of years younger and pretty cute. Curves in all the right places and we had fun. That's what it was, fun.

After that our calls and video calls became more and more raunchy, we shared fantasies and got off watching each other. The things you hear about but would never do. But we did it and it was exciting. I drove up to meet her for a while near her work and we spent some more time together and we played about and fumbled in the back of the car like teenagers but didn't go all the way. But by then we were lusting after each other and so we arranged to meet with one sole intention and that was to have sex. Neither of us had been unfaithful before but both wanted and needed this.

So, we met in a town between the two of our homes and went to a hotel that she had booked. We met in the town and went to the hotel together. Once in the room we opened some Prosecco and strawberries that I had brought, ate and drank some and then it happened. We were both very nervous and apprehensive but we soon relaxed and had the most amazing sex for hours and hours. It was incredible. Better than I could remember in such a long time and it was exactly what we both wanted. We showered, dressed and then went our separate ways home with big smiles on our faces.

That was not the end of it though, it was not a one off. We were still chatting and talking all the time. We had a connection that became beyond the original intention of just hooking up and it was no longer just about sex. Neither of us were the type of person who could do sex without any attachment at all and so this was now an affair, a relationship and not just sex. We were getting deeper and far beyond what we were expecting when it all started out. I drove up to see her and as it was summer and hot we had outdoor sex in a corn field with a picnic blanket on the ground.

Then she came down all the way to visit me at my house. We had sex all over the house which was absolutely incredible. You could not imagine or write this kind of thing and how amazing, risky and thrilling it was. After that we went for a bite to eat and a drink at a local pub and even drove around the town in her open top sports car and it was so dangerous and exiting. Someone I knew would sure see me and then Caroline would find out but that was the risk I wanted and did not think twice about it. I even hoped that would happen.

During this time, we both talked about leaving our partners and getting together properly. This was getting serious, but we agreed we needed to wait until things were all sorted, and we had a plan to do it properly with somewhere to live. We started looking at houses to rent and everything.

Then we met again at another hotel in a large town and had an amazing afternoon again of pure sex and pleasure. When it was time to leave Amy wanted us to not go home but to just stay together and leave our partners now that night. I wasn't ready at all but I had an ultimatum and so I reluctantly agreed. I was going to go home and get some clothes and things and tell Caroline that it was over, and I was leaving. So, I drove home just to do that with a steely determination. I could do it this time.

So, I arrived home very late and much later than expected. Caroline was not happy and demanding to know why I was so late. So, I told her that I had made my mind up to leave her and I had come to pack my bags and go. This did not go down well. She wanted to know why and kept pressing and asked me if I had someone else. She asked me the direct question and I told her that I was having an affair and I was going to leave and be with this other woman.

Again, she was not impressed. I packed a bag and put it in the car to leave. She got the kids together with her and told them that Daddy was leaving them and deserting them because he was having an affair and sex with another woman, a prostitute he had met online. The children were both crying, and she was playing the emotional guilt card to get to me and stop me leaving but I was having none of it.

When I tried to leave in the car she laid herself on the bonnet of the car and physically stopped me from driving away. She pleaded for me to come inside and talk with her. She pleaded and pleaded for me not to leave and had the kids there with her crying using every trick in the book to stop me leaving. And I fell for it again. She knew how to get me. Sitting the kids down in front of me and telling them I was leaving them. The emotional blackmail was just too much.

I called Amy and told her it was over, that I couldn't do it. That I couldn't leave and that we would have to stop all contact and everything. She was devastated. Like me, she was planning to leave her husband and had planned it in advance. She had packed a case and planned to stay at the hotel with me that night. It was now after 9pm and she had no option but to go home and try and explain where she had been. At first, she said she was coming to my house to get me and fight with Caroline. When Caroline heard this, she was angry that she knew where we lived and that meant she'd been to our house. Things just got worse.

I was in such a dilemma. I so wanted to be free. I thought I was in love with Amy, but I just could not walk out on my kids like that. It was all wrong. It had all gone wrong and was exactly not how I wanted it to go. Amy had pushed me into a corner and pushed me too hard for us to be together straight away, but I wasn't ready. I wasn't strong enough and I crumbled. Again, I was too weak.

I agreed to stay. I gave into the begging and promises again. The promises of change, the promises of no more abuse. The promise of starting again. The promise of forgiveness. Plus keeping the family together and not hurting or leaving the children. Another nightmare created by myself whereby I was going to suffer more.

The hold this woman had on me was incredible. I had become co-dependent on her and her abuse. Add that to the complete love for my kids and the need to protect them it was all just too much for me. The emotional blackmail got to me.

I called Amy and told her it was done, it was over, and I couldn't do it. I told her not to come and not to contact me again. I blocked her on my phone, Facebook and the apps we used to chat with. I tried to block her out of my mind and start again. It was tough and I acted cold and heartless. I had no more contact with Amy and have no idea what happened to her afterwards.

Love bombing.

The next few months were, as you can imagine, difficult. Caroline was love bombing me and was kind of trying to have sex with me except that it wasn't full sex because she wouldn't have actual intercourse with me until I had been given the all clear from the sexual health clinic. She wanted me tested for STD's and HIV before she would do it. So, I had to go and get tested and show her proof. She knew sex was the issue that caused this and so made sure she gave me some. Once I had the all clear we did have sex for a while. It was her form of control and power over me and she tried to use it fully. The way to a man's contentment is not only through his stomach in most cases.

The other thing that I had done was book a vasectomy. I made the decision that I didn't want any more children and that it would not be fair to my two if I did so I went and had it done a few weeks later. Caroline insisted in having sex with me even though it was just after the operation and I was sore. It felt like I was being raped. We had gone from one extreme to another just like she did previously when we were trying for a baby. She would be obsessed with getting pregnant, so we were at it all the time. I didn't complain. I later discovered that this was a tactic called 'love bombing' and is where the woman showers you with sex to hook you in and get you back under her control. Then right enough as the textbook said she started withdrawing sex and using it to control me again.

During the weeks after the split with Amy, she tried to get in touch with me by every means possible. She even contacted my work office and left messages. I had to ask them to tell her not to call again. She sent me messages on various platforms that we had not communicated before and I was sure she was going to turn up at our house at some point. She stalked me at work and things but never came to our home that I am aware of and I never spoke with her again. To this day I have no idea what happened to her and how she is. To think I was ready to run away and start a new life with her yet I cut her out completely. What a low life I was.

Then Caroline insisted that we go to a marriage counselling organisation for some marriage counselling. There was a catch though, she would not let me or her mention anything to do with the domestic abuse or violence she had inflicted on me. She knew that if this was mentioned a whole can of worms and a different perspective on everything would be taken. When we went, the lady asked why we had come, and Caroline said, "we are here because he had an affair with a tart off the internet". It didn't start well. She just wanted the counsellor to tell me how wrong I was and what I needed to do to fix everything, something she had been saying to me since it all happened.

The counsellor did not work like that though and she wanted to hear both sides, so I told her mine and she gave her balanced opinions and advice and gave us some things to work with. Caroline was not pleased afterwards and said the whole thing was a waste of time but agreed to carry it forward for the 6 sessions we had booked and paid for. Her only intention was to get backing from the counsellor to help her make my life hell. Something she had been doing all along. She was now the victim and not me. It made no matter what she had done to me I had hurt her, I was the bad one and that meant I had to make up for it. So, for months I suffered. She made me do everything and if I said anything she just shouted at me and told me to go and live with the whore I found on the internet.

The counselling continued, and we tried the suggested things to bring us closer and she was told to forgive me and move on so eventually we did. After a while we did return to normal which meant the abuse, and everything was back. Again, I was back where I started.

I had tried another drastic method of escaping her tyranny but her hold on me and my dependency on her was just too much. I blamed her for everything I was feeling and experiencing. I saw her as the reason for my misery.

I now realise that this was not true. It was my perceived reality but not the actual reality. My situation was not the cause of my unhappiness rather it was how I was thinking and processing it all in my head. Always dreading what she would do next and getting anxious about it before it even happened. I was living with an outside in approach and not an inside out one.

I was believing what she said about me to be true however it was not true. It was only her opinion and thoughts about me.

I did suffer a lot from anxiety and depression at this stage and had to get help from my doctor. I was prescribed some anti-anxiety drugs and they worked very well on me. They took the edge off the pain and calmed me down a lot.

They allowed me to cope with what she threw at me and not react in the same way. I was calmer and was able to function better at work and in normal life. Many don't get on well with the medication but for me it was the best thing.

I saw how anxious and depressed I had been in recent years. How at times I had self-harmed myself and thought about another form of escape. The most drastic one, about suicide. But I was not so far gone to do more than think about it fleetingly.

Escape Plan.

Wind on yet again another year and it got very bad again. It was the same as always and I knew I needed to get out, that fact never changed. I re-joined my support network and decided I was going to leave her. I wasn't going to try the court route. I just planned to follow the standard leave and get divorced one. So, at the start of 2016 I was ready to put plans in place. I felt like I was strong enough to do it this time. This time there was no other person involved and I had no intention, it would be just about me and the kids.

The network of support I had from my online forum seemed better than before and my job, working for myself on flexible contracts, allowed me the flexibility to be able to look after the kid's part time. I was in a much better position overall. I looked for a suitable house in the local area, so I would be close to the kids but far enough from her to be able to live in peace. I didn't want to move away from the kids but be close and hoped to share custody thus gaining the best of both worlds.

I had some funds available and decided the best way was to set myself up in a new home in secret and move out once it was all ready. I thought this was the best approach as that she would not be able to stop me because it would be already done and dusted. It was also the advice given from my network as they knew she would try everything to stop me if she knew anything in advance. Once out I could file for divorce and sort the rest out while secure in my new place and away from her. Not only that but a safe and peaceful place where the kids had a choice to come whenever they wanted because it would be very close for them for school and everything else.

I found a really nice three bedroomed detached house in a village two miles away from Richmond. It was walkable from the main town and on Sacha's bus route home from school in the city. One room for each of the kids and a master room for me. It had a garage and a conservatory too plus a kids play area and park just across the street. It was perfect. I rented it and bought furniture for it. I took loads of things from the garage that were old and due to be thrown out but for months I kept them all ready for this point. I had been thinking about this for a long time. It was a perfect plan.

I got the keys and started setting it up. I set up the home office first and started working from there during the day whilst I worked out the best time to move out and move in. I loved going there and working in complete peace and tranquillity. Then I did something for myself and rather crazy. Call it a mid-life crisis but I went and bought myself a little convertible sports car. It was a British racing green MG convertible and so much fun. It was 10 years old and a modern classic and I loved it.

For about a month I would spend my days in my new home setting things up and working there. Going out for spins in my sports car and just being free. It was so good. I spoke with Sacha and told her what I was planning. I took her to the house and she was super excited. She knew me and her mum splitting up was the best thing for all of us and having somewhere she could choose to come to at any point was what she needed. Just like I did. I even took her out for a spin in the Barchetta. It was exactly what Sacha needed.

It was going to be perfect. The only thing left to do was to tell Caroline and move out. Simple.

Except it's never that simple is it? I was advised by the group not to tell her face to face. Not to give her the chance to stop me or make me change my mind. So, I followed the advice and sent her an email telling her I had moved out and it was over. I was filing for divorce and that was it.

Then she started calling and calling and leaving messages. I ignored them. She replied to my email and said that her mother had just been diagnosed with cancer that day and she needed me. I sat there on my own in the empty house and felt so bad. I felt alone and it all felt wrong. I didn't know why it just didn't feel right. So, I jumped in the car and headed back 'home'. I knocked on the door and she greeted me with tears and open arms. Distraught about her mother and just wanting me back and our family together.

I had crumbled again.

We talked, she made the same old promises and I fell for it all again. I felt so useless and worthless again. Everything she said I was I had become. Sacha was confused and didn't know what to make of the whole thing. I was confused myself. Caroline wanted me to get rid of the house but although I said I would at first, I didn't. I was still hanging on to it. Hanging on to the dream of being free from her and able to live my life like a normal person. Eventually and reluctantly after a few more weeks of her demands I did instruct the estate agents to see if they could find another tenant.

She made me take her to the house to see it. She said it was a nice house but managed to criticise most of the things I had bought for it. Luckily, I had not built up most of the flat packed furniture yet and the things I had unpacked I was able to repack. I had ordered everything online, so I was able to just return it all or most of it. The bit that was so funny though was when I took her around the house and showed her it all she was shocked at how advanced and prepared I had been. Then I took her to the garage and said I have one more thing to show you. One more confession to make.

She thought I was going to show her a new bicycle or something but when I opened the garage door and showed her the sports car she went really mad. Accusing me of being selfish and of having a midlife crisis. She was not happy, and I was going to suffer but it was so funny, and I was trying not to laugh. She told me I had to sell it. Eventually, months later, I did, and part exchanged it for a new family car which she then took to be her own saying it was payback. Her mother had an operation and recovered from her cancer and all was well. Or was it?

Payback ensued for the next months and continued much longer for my bad behaviour. Then as predicted it all went back to the same old rubbish of control and abuse. Again, I had tried to escape. Again, I had failed. I was too weak, too indoctrinated in her rubbished. Too conditioned to what was normal for me even though it was awful. Better the devil you know eh? I thought all women were going to be the same, just like her. Her telling me that the grass is never greener on the other side started to stick with me and I was stuck. Future events would however totally disprove this theory.

A few months later I got a new contract, working full time an hour or so away and so that meant I was around at home so much less. It was an escape for me. Another outlet to help cope and survive with everything. However, I never let go of my dream to be free. I still thought about it. I still wanted it. I still desperately wanted to leave her and be free, but I doubted myself so much. The contract I had turned into a really good permanent role with a great package. It meant I had the means to escape and could move near to my work and far away from her. That's the dream I held onto.

This dream kept me going each day. I kept looking at houses to rent near my work. I think that time I had changed, I had not caved in completely. Yes, I had yet again failed to escape but I had a taste of freedom and had not yet given up hope. I had not lost my desire to be free and it kept me going. Her attitude and demand always got in the way of my career and that would never change.

Life is too short.

So, let's fast forward again. It's now the summer of 2017 and at the start of June my mother was taken into hospital with some stomach pains. Those pains turned out to be cancer and it had spread too far and so she was diagnosed as terminal. They didn't really know how long she had but we were looking at possibly a year if she came through an operation to remove the tumour. This was a real shock but the way my parents were handling it and their positive attitude was so inspiring.

I went over to visit her and it was a nice surprise for her. The hospital needed a couple of weeks to get her into a good strong position for the operation. She was looking very well and in good spirits. My mum and dad had taken the news very well and remained positive, one step at a time. Caroline was at first quite supportive and sympathetic, but it soon wore off. Going to visit my mum meant more work for her and so it became a problem and she made it plainly clear. Her support was tentative at best focussing just on its effect on herself.

My mum had her operation and came through it. She made it passed the initial hurdle and I was back and forth to Wales to see her as much as I could. Caroline was not supportive most of the time. One time I had a call from my dad saying that Mum had taken a turn for the worst and they said she wasn't going to make it through the night. So, I jumped in my car and drove up to Wales. She had pneumonia and despite what they thought she pulled through that night and was then stable. I spent a week up there with my dad and her until she seemed stable enough, so I then went back home, although she never quite recovered her full strength after that.

Then one night a week or so later I had a call from my dad at 10pm. He had been called back to the hospital because Mum had taken a turn for the worse and they feared she was not going to make it and this time they seemed sure. The dialysis she had been having for her kidney failure was taking a lot out of her on top of everything else.

I again jumped in the car and headed South. I was due to be visiting the Midlands for work the next day for work, so I said I'd drive to there and call my dad to see how things were when I got that far.

I called him around midnight and he said she had stabilised and they thought she was ok that I should stop where I am for now for the night and see how it looked in the morning. So, I looked for a hotel but could not get one anywhere. Every hotel was either shut for the night or fully booked. I decided in the end after about two hours of searching to settle down and sleep in back of the car.

I just dropped off to sleep when I had a call from my dad at 3.02am. He said, "I'm sorry son but your mum has just gone, she has just slipped away". I just jumped in the front of the car and headed West as fast as I dared.

I could not believe it and I just was shouting "no please God no, don't let this be the case, not my poor little Mum not without allowing me to say goodbye". I prayed like I had never prayed before and drove like I'd never driven before.

Then at 3.41am Dad called me back and said, "You are never going to believe this, but your mum has come back, do you want to talk to her?" and put her on the phone. I could not believe it. My mum said hello and I told her to hang on till I got there. I drove like a maniac and was there at the hospital within a few hours.

That night my prayers had been answered and it was the start of my journey back to Christ and renewing my flagging faith in God.

When I got to Mum she was so pleased to see me and was able to talk. I was so thankful for this opportunity and although I knew time would be limited, it was such a blessing to have that extra time with her.

My dad explained that three doctors were present and they pronounced her dead just before he called me. He said my mum's body was stone cold all over apart from a small bit of warmth at the top of her head. Then she just started breathing again. My dad saw it and told them he thought she was breathing again and right enough she was. She had come back. It was a miracle. The medical staff could not offer any rational explanation as to what had just occurred. It was a real-life miracle witnessed first-hand by my dad, a non-religious man, and he said it was divine intervention.

After that I stayed up there for the next two weeks with my dad and sister with all of us by her bed with her. After the first day or so any time I spoke with Caroline all she seemed interested in was when I was coming home and complaining about the kids. The more I was away and the more she nagged me the more I resented her. I talked during this time with my mum. I opened my heart to her. I told her how unhappy I was and that I planned to leave Caroline and she was actually very happy about it. She said she wished I had left her years ago and that she hated the way she treated me. She told me to go and be happy. That day I made a promise to my mum that I would do just that and she need not worry any longer.

Over the next weeks Mum grew weaker and eventually passed away. In total it was only 8 weeks from diagnosis to death. I had gone home when we knew the time was close and she had gone home to die. I took the kids over to see her two days before she died which was so tough. On the day she died I was at home. I got the call at about 9.30am from my dad. I spent that whole morning just emptying the loft of rubbish and filling a skip. I could have, well a normal husband would have, called my wife at work and told her my mother had died but I didn't. When

Caroline came home I was sat in the living room drinking a vodka and coke. She came in the door and glared at me. Then shouted at me saying "why are you drinking again" and stormed off upstairs.

It was not until much later that I told her my mum had died. She didn't care, and I no longer cared for her. I hated her, and I was going to fulfil my promise to my mother to be happy. I put things in motion and looked for a place to live near my work.

That is what I did.

The Escape.

I put plans into place and found somewhere to live nearby my work. I even found someone who wanted to share it and after much wrangling and procrastinating I eventually first moved out in November.

This time I did it and escaped.

This time I stayed strong and saw it through. It had taken me 5 years and three failed attempts from first realising the situation to getting out.

It was not that easy or straightforward. The hold she had on me and my love for my kids still pulled me back there. When Christmas came she wanted me to come 'home' and not to leave the kids without their dad for Christmas. She said maybe we could see how it went and I might reconsider. I had no intention of reconsidering but then I did have a track record of caving in.

So, I went back for Christmas and New Year. It was good to be with the children, but it was not good nor peaceful. She wanted me to sleep in the marital bed, but I refused. She also said she wanted sex but again I refused and stayed in my room at the other end of the house. This was an opportunity for her to show all her best qualities, she does have some, but she carried on with her usual shouting, demands and arguments. It was not fun.

I was not going back. I was still leaving but in the short term she and the kids needed some support from me and I was happy to spend time away at my place but also spend some time there with them.

Then on the 28th of December I met a woman on a dating site that I had registered with. As I had moved out I wanted to also move on and so dating was the next step. Since I moved out in November I'd been out on a few dates and was just finding my feet.

This time though this woman and I just really hit it off. We were from different backgrounds but we both embraced that completely. We talked and talked, video chatted and the more we talked the more we fell for each other. We had our first date and it was amazing and from there one thing led to another.

This new relationship and the support from her gave me the strength and confidence to completely break free and move out fully. I did it and honoured the promise I had made to my mother. By rights, this woman and I should never have come across each other, again I believe it was down to divine intervention. God had a plan for me and set me on a new path and this lady was a very good Christian.

The result.

So, winding on a little further to now. I didn't go back. I stayed strong and I honoured the promise to my Mother.

The woman I met via the online dating site is now my wife. We were married and living together within 8 months of my leaving.

We have the most amazing marriage and relationship together. We have both been through difficult marriages. We don't argue, our lives are peaceful, and we are blessed. We try to help others who have been through tough relationships or are stuck in one. We have a blended interracial family with children from previous marriages that makes us unique. We like to travel and attend many events and have fun. We even have a business together.

I am happy, confident and secure. I found that the grass can be greener on the other side.

My wife helped in bringing my faith to the fore. I was always a believer and a Christian, but I have encountered God now very deeply. I was baptised by full immersion and we put God at the centre of our lives.

Our marriage, our support for each other and our trust in God will stand us in good stead no matter what challenges life continues to throw at us. Other challenges have also been overcome in recent times but that's a story for another book I think.

I have very little contact with Caroline since I left. The few times we have been face to face or talked on the phone has resulted in an abusive torrent pouring out of her and so I will not meet her face to face or take any calls from her. We communicate mostly via email and only in relation to the children, especially about Alice. That way she has no or little opportunity to try and manipulate me. No contact is the best route with this type of person.

I see Alice every Friday after school and work and every second weekend she comes and stays at our house for two nights. Even though he is still at her mother's we have a great relationship and we have good quality time together.

Sacha is another story entirely. She suffered a lot through the years, far more than Alice, and I let her down. If I had managed to escape earlier, then it would have been so much better for

Sacha. She has been exposed to her mother's conditioning and seems to have become like her mother in some ways. My worst fear. Her worst fear.

At first when I left Sacha was ok with it but when I met my new wife she took great upset at this and has refused to talk with me or meet me since. Despite this I love her and care for her deeply and she will be welcomed into my life whenever she wants to. It is with sadness I think about how I tried to love and protect her for all those years, yet she still came out of it so badly damaged.

This experience has made me stronger and I hope that it will help, encourage or inspire someone never to accept what is not right. Never to give up and always look forward.

What is domestic abuse?

It is often thought that domestic abuse only relates to being physically attacked or abused in some way, but this simply not the case. There are several types of domestic abuse and each is harmful to the victim.

Physical abuse.

This covers everything from slaps, punches, kicking that can cause cuts and bruises, burns and in some rare situations, death. The extent of the violence does not have actually to leave any marks or bruises to be categorised as physical abuse. Actions such as the pulling of hair or manhandling to the ground for instance, are also classed as physical abuse.

Emotional abuse.

To be a victim of abuse it is not necessary to have suffered physical abuse from a partner. When emotional abuse is involved then victims often think that they are not being abused or worry that they will not be taken seriously if they speak out or try to deal with it.

Emotional methods are often used by a person, the abuser, to destroy a victim's self-esteem and confidence and create a situation whereby they can be controlled or coerced more easily. The abuser may criticise them, try to isolate them from friends and family, force them to give up work or change careers. They sometime try to humiliate them in front of people and they often try to put the person down.

Over a prolonged period, this will reduce the victim's confidence and self-esteem until they become reliant, co-dependent or scared of their partner. This then gives the abuser the ability to control them.

Financial abuse.

This can be a powerful form of abuse and is often why victims feel trapped with no way out of the situation because they have no or limited access to funds. The abuser may take control of all finances, they may stop them from earning independently or working, and will often monitor their spending.

Sexual abuse and control.

No person should be or feel that they are forced into any kind of sexual activity. Being in a relationship or marriage does not permit automatic consent for sex. If a person is made to feel threatened or coerced into sexual activity, that is a form of abuse.

In addition, using sex to control a person is also a form of abuse. Much like financial abuse this involves controlling when and if sex happens. Forms of this involve withholding sex as a punishment or for some other reason. Using sex as a reward for doing things the victim does not want to do, a form of coercion.

What to do if you are suffering

If in doubt, get out:

I hope anyone who reads this and is in a similar situation, does not make the mistakes I made. If it's bad and you have tried to make it work but it has not, then get out. If someone hurts you or your children, then get out. There are several good organisations that can support both men and women to extricate themselves safely from such situations.

A simple Google search for "domestic abuse help" or words to that effect will bring up national and local support organisations but remember to clear your browsing history if you believe your abuser is going to access your web history.

For men in the UK Mankind is the best and only real place to go http://www.mankind.org.uk/

For women in the UK Womens Aid is prominent: https://www.womensaid.org.uk/

Always keep your hope:

There is always the chance to start again and be happy, don't stay where you are not happy. Everyone deserves to be happy and can be happy. There is love after divorce. There is a possibility of a second chance at life. Take it because life is too short to be unhappy.

If you are struggling to deal with the mental pressure:

If you are in a really tough place and thinking about suicide or self-harm, then please seek support. There are many organisations out there that can support men and women going through mental struggles. You can also go and see your doctor or GP and explain what is going on. There should be no shame in seeking help. Mental illness is an illness and it can be treated.

In the UK the most prominent organisation is Mind
https://www.mind.org.uk/

What is Narcissistic Personality Disorder (NPD)

I think many will have heard of the term Narcissist. It often gets used when someone seems to be very self-centred but when you encounter a person with Narcissistic Personality Disorder or NPD as its referred as, then the stakes and risks are on a different level.

Narcissists can be quite hard to spot. They understand how to manipulate and control their victims and manage to do this without most people realising.

What makes it even harder and can be confusing for the victim is that they don't all act in exactly the same way and can act differently at different times. Some behaviours are a consistent feature of the different types such as idealising, devaluing, and then treating their partners badly. It is commonly understood that there are different types of narcissists who don't act the same outwardly.

The main common traits of a narcissist are:

- Have issues with their own self-esteem
- Very self-centered and focussed on themselves
- They have a lack empathy for others
- Very sensitive to perceived criticism
- Have a bad temper and get angry easily
- They Devalue others putting them down
- Very conscious of their status and how they are seen by others

What are the types of narcissist and how to spot them?

There are commonly defined into 3 types that are similar in some ways bud different in others:

1. Covert or Closet Narcissist
2. Exhibitionist Narcissist
3. Toxic Narcissist

Covert Narcissist

Sometimes called also a Closet Narcissist, they like to be in a relationship with a person that they can idealise as special. They feed off that person's status and think it makes them better. They can be uncomfortable when the spotlight is directly on them as they are conflicted.

They have often earned from childhood that they will be attacked if they seek admiration themselves because they have often come from as family with a Narcissist parent or sibling who devalued them as they were thought of as competition. Their narcissistic traits were hidden to protect themselves from the parent and were only praised when they praised the parent.

Often Closet Narcissists are quite insecure and feel vulnerable if they are the centre of attention. They fear others can see their flaws and devalue them like the Narcissistic parent. So sometimes they get involved with people, causes, religions, and other things that they think are special and will make them look good via association.

They are not always overly demanding, but they manipulate situations to get their own way or what they want. Making themselves the victim and use your empathy make you do what they want you to do. They put op a pretence of being nice when they are not and its not at all how they feel in themselves.

Many Covert Narcissists let themselves to be used by others and work hard for things and people they admire to look good.

Exhibitionist Narcissist

They very insensitive and controlling and come across initially as perhaps bossy. They expect everyone to look up to them and agree with whatever they say or want. Any form of non-agreement is perceived as criticism and is dismissed and devalued. They require continual reassurance and ego boosts confirming they are perfect, amazing and always right.

They like to be the centre of attention and always want to dominate conversations and situations. They have a sense of entitlement to being treated as if they are so special. They can act with complete confidence. Can be excellent at telling stories and handing out their advice even if it isn't asked for. When they feel insecure, they get angry easily and like to put the person in their sights down and often in the most awful way.

No matter what happens they believe they are better than everyone else, that they are perfect and know everything. They expect those around them to submit with their point of view because they are always right. They have a real superiority complex and so everyone else is just rubbish.

This arrogance is just a façade and not how they really feel inside. Therefore, it is easy to disrupt and break their self-image. This makes Exhibitionist Narcissists react very badly and excessively to even minor critism. They are very quick to anger and will start a fight over simple things that most people might not even think anything of. They can also be vicious and cruel to those around them as they lack and time of empathy or emotional stability.

They like to brag and tell stories about their amazing achievements but then put down and devalue anyone who dares to disagree with them. They will make fun of someone very cruelly and don't care if they can hear or not. They like to tell people how fat, stupid, useless, ugly, dumb they are.

They have little sympathy or even awareness for other people's upset, feelings or reactions to their behaviour. They are so blinded by their own superiority they think everyone thinks they are amazing.

Toxic Narcissist

They establish themselves as superior to you and try to make you feel that you are not good enough. You would spend your whole time with them being put down and devalued. You will never be able to please them or make them happy. They never never give you any praise for anything you have done or achieved, instead they criticise and pull you down. Any confidence in yourself that you may have had when you met them gets ground down and replaced with anxiety and self-doubt.

Toxic Narcissists are "crazy" and are not content with just being the centre of attention, they want to dominate all around them. They can be often be sadistic and seem to actually enjoy hurting other people not just physically but also mentally. They need you to submit to their way and be scared of them.

Some have a real chip on their shoulders about the fact that they cannot attain their own unrealistic expectations of themselves. They are jealous of anybody who has success or happiness that they believe they should have and seem bent on destroying other people's happiness. This relates more to those closest to them including partner, there own parents and even their children.

They are poisonous and act just like a bully, sometimes you can easily think they are a psychopath. They will try and publicly humiliate people where they think they can get away from it but always humiliate people when they are one on one. They store any little thing you have done and rake it up and beat you up about out over and over again without remorse.

Toxic Narcissists can also act like a Covert Narcissist at times, dropping in little digs with a smile to rile you and get you angry. They can also act very nice at times which reels you back in under a false sense of security then – bam, they got you.

If you think you may be in a relationship with a narcissist then my advice is to get out as soon as you can.

How to get out – Planning and Support.

1. Seek help and support (see previous chapter).

    - There are organisations that can help, use them.
    - Use any friends or family support networks you have but always be careful who you can and cannot trust.

2. Gather evidence over a period of time.

    - Keep a log or diary as I did with records of what happened and when.
    - Keep notes and any evidence, photos of injuries etc.
    - Visit the doctor and record and injuries sustained.

3. Research how to make and escape plan.

    - Many of the websites that support domestic abuse victims offer details on how to plan your escape.
    - Research these or Google – "how to escape an abusive relationship".

- Think about what the best and safest way for you might be to get out and whose support you will need.

- Remember to be careful in deleting or covering your search history on the device you use so as the abuser is not able to access what you have been researching.

4. Make your own escape plan.

- Plan it in secret and get support to see it through

5. Follow the escape plan through when the time is right.

- Make sure you are prepared and ready, that the support you need is in place. Get your ducks in a row and then go for it.

- Try not to make the mistake I made, I was unable to break free on many occasions, and stay out.

6. Afterwards - Limit contact as much as possible and go no contact if you can.

- This is where I failed in my first attempts, I gave the opportunity to be persuaded and convinced to return.

- You cannot reason with these people and so no contact is best, never face to face and use email as much as possible. This is what has worked for me when I finally got out and is still working for me.

7. File for divorce or any legal action you wish to take.

- Once the dust is settled and you are secure in a safe place then consider how you want to proceed.
- File for divorce, custody of the children or whatever legal process suits your situation.

8. Stay calm and in control at all times.

- Don't let the abuser get to you and try not to react or overthink any of the situation. It was not your fault.

- Once you have left remember you are no longer a victim, it's in the past you are a survivor.

- Don't look back, be free and get on with your life, the future can be so much brighter.

44951991R00130

Printed in Poland
by Amazon Fulfillment
Poland Sp. z o.o., Wrocław